T0165604

KINGDOM LIVING…

WALKING,
RUNNING,
FIGHTING,
TRUSTING,
PRAYING

Dr. George W. Mitchell

WestBow
PRESS
A DIVISION OF THOMAS NELSON

Copyright © 2013 Dr. George W. Mitchell.

All rights reserved. No part of this book may be used or reproduced by any means, graphic, electronic, or mechanical, including photocopying, recording, taping or by any information storage retrieval system without the written permission of the publisher except in the case of brief quotations embodied in critical articles and reviews.

Scripture quotations taken from the New American Standard Bible®, Copyright © 1960, 1962, 1963, 1968, 1971, 1972, 1973, 1975, 1977, 1995 by The Lockman Foundation. Used by permission." (www.Lockman.org)

Scripture quotations marked (*AB*) taken from the Amplified Bible, Copyright © 1954, 1958, 1962, 1964, 1965, 1987 by The Lockman Foundation. Used by permission.

WestBow Press books may be ordered through booksellers or by contacting:

WestBow Press
A Division of Thomas Nelson
1663 Liberty Drive
Bloomington, IN 47403
www.westbowpress.com
1 (866) 928-1240

Because of the dynamic nature of the Internet, any web addresses or links contained in this book may have changed since publication and may no longer be valid. The views expressed in this work are solely those of the author and do not necessarily reflect the views of the publisher, and the publisher hereby disclaims any responsibility for them.

Any people depicted in stock imagery provided by Thinkstock are models, and such images are being used for illustrative purposes only. Certain stock imagery © Thinkstock.

ISBN: 978-1-4908-1396-7 (sc)
ISBN: 978-1-4908-1395-0 (hc)
ISBN: 978-1-4908-1397-4 (e)

Library of Congress Control Number: 2013919452

Printed in the United States of America.

WestBow Press rev. date: 12/13/2013

To my children, Caleb, Stephen, and Esther and to their spouses, Elisa, Erin, and Clark, all of whom are constantly challenging me to live my life according to the principles described in this book. I am thankful for all that they have shown me by living their own lives before me and by calling upon me to check my own words and actions to see whether they match up to kingdom living or not. Their ways of dealing with me have not always been pleasant. However, I am always assured that their greater intention is to demonstrate their love for me and their desire for me to live according to truth in order to honor our King above all else. Their lives are very precious to me, and I am continually grateful for them.

Contents

Introduction

As I walk'd through the wilderness of this world, I lighted
on a certain place, where was a Denn; And I laid me down
in that place to sleep: And as I slept I dreamed a Dream. I
dreamed and behold *I saw a Man clothed with Raggs, standing
in a certain place with his face from his own House, a Book in
his hand, and a great burden on his back.* I looked and saw him
open the Book, and Read therein; and as he Read, he wept and
trembled: and not being able longer to contain, he brake out
with a lamentable cry; saying, *what shall I do?*

This quote comes from that classic piece of literature, *The Pilgrims
Progress* by John Bunyan (Oxford World's Classics, Oxford
University Press, ed. by W. R. Owens, revised 2008, p. 10). The
question at the end is one that all of us ask on a regular basis,
either consciously or unconsciously: "What shall I do?" What am
I to do as I live this life on a daily basis? What shall I do in light
of the situation I am faced with right now? How do I proceed in
this life?

Robert J. Morgan has said, "Stress and worry break us
down. They are the unseen source of our headaches, backaches,
heartaches, and bellyaches. They produce every thing from obesity
to obscenity, from constipation to diarrhea, and from impatience
to impotence. They give us knotted stomachs, sleepless nights,

high blood pressure, low morale. They make our tempers short and our days long. They cause indigestion, irritation, chest pain, and muscle strain" (*Nelson's Complete Book of Stories, Illustrations, and Quotes,* ed. by Thomas Nelson Publishers, Nashville, 2000, p. 801).

Let's face it! Life is not a "bowl of cherries." Not everyone even likes cherries. It is also not a "bed of roses." In fact, roses have thorns. At the same time, life isn't what the old *Hee Haw* song says either: "Gloom, despair, and agony on me; deep, dark depression, excessive misery."

As *The Pilgrim's Progress* points out, life is a "pilgrimage" or journey. We are going from one place to another. There is a destination. There is an end or goal that we have in sight that motivates us to continue. Now, here is the tricky part. The goal or end is all about one's perspective. Or maybe it would be better to call it one's belief system.

Think with me for a moment. Let's propose that there exists a personal, infinite God who created the world and all that is within it. If this God really is God, He possesses all knowledge and all truth. Being infinite, He recognizes that the finite creatures He has made need a revelation from Him that they can understand. So He communicates His mind and will to them in a written form to show them how they can know Him and how they should live in the world in which He has placed them.

What a glorious concept! How great would it be to know the certainty of reality and to learn how to understand it. Of course, this is exactly the guidance that the Bible claims to provide. It is God's Word, the written declaration of truth to us. There is nothing like it. There is no other book like it. Read it and compare it to all other books!

Of course, there is another way of looking at things. We could take the position that everything we have before us in this world just happened, by chance or by a cataclysmic explosion.

Everything is just a great coming-together of atoms, and we are nothing more than a higher form of animal, evolved from the slime of the earth. Or we are sophisticated machines without any meaning or purpose except to live out a sad and doomed existence on the planet. With this particular system of belief, there is no hope of ever coming to any conclusion about real truth, so we must live the best we can and do whatever we can to make our presence here bearable and somewhat enjoyable.

These are two basic belief systems. Of course, there are variations of each one, but basically there are only two. We are either going to live our lives believing that there is a personal, infinite God who is there and has revealed Himself to us, or that there is *no* God, and even if there is, that we can't know anything about Him or that He is in many ways just like us—and doesn't care anything about us anyway.

The position of this book is that God does exist and that He has declared truth to us and has given us a written communication that tells us who He is, who we are, how we can know Him, how we should live, and that there is an end goal, a destination for our lives. Pilgrim's basic question, "What shall I do?," is answered within the pages of God's Word.

Even if this is not your belief system, I would encourage you to keep reading. Maybe you will begin to think differently about your own life. If you really believe that you are here by accident— that the beauty and grandeur around you, all your experiences, and the birth of newborn babies just happen—then maybe you have been too quick to listen to the naysayers and have not spent enough time alone honestly saying, "Lord God, if You are really there, make Yourself known to me. Show me who You are. Speak to my heart."

We need to take one more step and consider this: not only has the living God of the universe made Himself known to us in the written language of His Word, but He has also made Himself known to us through the living Word, the Lord Jesus Christ. If you want to know how great and awesome the God of the heavens and the earth is, then look no further than Jesus Christ. Read the gospels of Matthew, Mark, Luke, and John. Let Jesus Christ overwhelm you with His love, grace, mercy, gentleness, humility, majesty, glory, and utter greatness.

So, this is what we are going to do. We are going to let God tell us how we should live by examining His revelation to us. Of course, this will not be an exhaustive study that brings to our attention all that God's Word says. We will seek to look at a few basic ideas and concepts to help us on our way in this life. Before we can begin this journey, there are a few things we need to consider.

In order to start, continue, and complete the road before us, we need a power source to help us through every step we take. We need an inner source of strength to enable us to do what God requires. God's "book of directions" clearly indicates that we have all initially made gods that we worship. They may be the gods of pleasure, knowledge, riches, power, or—most of the time— ourselves. We cannot even begin to take the journey God has prepared for us if we are worshipping something or someone else.

Since our hearts or inner selves are following after false gods, our hearts must be changed. In Ezekiel 36:26–27, God says, "I will give you a new heart and put a new spirit within you; and I will remove the heart of stone from your flesh and give you a heart of flesh. And I will put My Spirit within you and cause you to walk in My statutes, and you will be careful to observe My ordinances" (All Scripture quotes, unless otherwise noted, are from the *Updated New American Standard Bible*, Zondervan, 1999).

This is what we need to begin our journey aright. We are all on a trip. The question is: where are we going? If we want to go where God wants us to go, we must have this new heart. We must have His Spirit dwelling in us to be able to move through this life and come to the end where we are destined to go. Jesus Christ is the one who gives us that new heart and puts His Spirit within us. As we acknowledge that we are idolaters, worshipping other gods, and that this is our very nature, we will want to change, to cast ourselves upon Jesus Christ and entrust ourselves to Him. Then we are "in Christ" and a "new creature: the old things passed away; behold new things have come" (2 Corinthians 5:17).

We now have the very Spirit of Christ living in us. This is our power. In order to live in this world, we must have a great energy source that will enable us to do the mundane things each day without grumbling, complaining, or becoming discouraged— and to do the great things, enduring hardship, suffering, and affliction. We cannot do this in our own strength. When we are born into this world, we begin to die. We are weak, frail individuals. Even our physical bodies declare to us that we need a power greater than ourselves. Spiritually, we are dead and must be given life by the power of God Himself.

Next, we must know where we are going. Again, our perspective must be based on what God says about this life. The world says that we are all headed for oblivion, "so let us eat, drink, and be merry, for tomorrow we may die" (1 Corinthians 15:32; Isaiah 22:13). If you really look at yourself and others and think that man, in all of his uniqueness, is just going to pass into nothingness, then it's possible that you haven't really considered who you are.

In God's written revelation to us, we are told that we are headed for "a new heavens and a new earth" (Isaiah 65:17; Revelation 21:1). This is going to be a place where God declares: "Behold, the tabernacle of God is among men, and He will dwell among them, and they shall be His people, and God Himself will be among them, and He will wipe away every tear from their eyes; and there will no longer be any death; there will no longer be any mourning, or crying, or pain; the first things have passed away" (Revelation 21:3–4).

According to God's Word, there are two destinations. One is this glorious heaven and earth that is going to replace the one we are living in presently. It is going to "come down" and take this earth's place (Revelation 21:2). This place will be for those who have the Spirit of God living in them.

However, there is another place for those who are still worshipping false gods. It is also characterized by being eternal. "For the cowardly and unbelieving and abominable and murderers and immoral persons and sorcerers and idolaters and all liars, their part will be in the lake that burns with fire and brimstone" (Revelation 21:8). I know we don't like to hear this, and many would say that we should not speak of this or talk like this or scare people or present God in this way. But, beloved, I must be honest with you so that you will really consider the truth. God has revealed that this is the reality of what is to come.

Finally, we need to realize that there are all kinds of dangers that we will meet along the way as we proceed through this life. In *The Pilgrim's Progress*, "Mr. Worldly Wiseman" told Pilgrim—who was headed for the "Wicket-gate," which would lead him to the "Celestial City"—that "Evangelist" had given him poor counsel about the way he was going. "There is not a more dangerous and troublesome way in the world, than is that unto which he hath directed thee … Thou hast met with something … already; for I see the dirt of the Slow (Slough) of Dispond (Despond) is upon thee; but that Slow is the beginning of the sorrows that do attend those that go on in that way: hear me … thou art like to meet with in the way which thou goest, Wearisomeness, Painfulness,

Hunger, Perils, Nakedness, Sword, Lions, Dragons, Darkness; and in a word death, and what not."

There were many other things that confronted Pilgrim: the Hill Difficulty, Vanity Fair, Obstinate, Pliable, Timorous, Mistrust, Apollyon (the foul Fiend), and so on. However, he also encountered Evangelist, Faithful, Interpreter, Patience, Hopeful, Great-Grace, Great-Heart, and so on.

It is important to understand that as we are going through this life, all kinds of triumphs and joys as well as great sorrows and struggles are going to come our way. None of us knows what tomorrow will bring. Therefore, it becomes the priority of our lives to know how we should live. What should we do? How can we prepare for what we cannot see? How do we face the journey?

Remember, this book takes the position that we have a personal, infinite God who has created us and loves us in His Son, Jesus Christ. He has given us a written record to show us how we are to approach our daily pilgrimage. In light of what the almighty, glorious, eternal God tells us, let's begin the journey.

Chapter 1

Walking

I have three great children, two boys and a girl. Actually, they are no longer children; they are two grown men and one beautiful young woman. When they were toddlers, I remember the excitement of seeing each of them learn to walk. Watching them fall and get up and fall and get up, until they finally took the first couple of wobbly steps, never grew old. Walking was something that they had to accomplish—or forever remain children. Sadly, not everyone is born into this world with the physical capacity to walk. However, for those who are, it would be a tragedy not to do so.

Our journey takes us through each day, one step at a time, as we traverse the daily routines of our lives. This walk involves physical exertion, but more importantly, we are talking about the inner walk that we take in our thoughts, feelings, and choices—our inner man, if you will. This is where the real walking takes place. We need to keep in mind how we are to view this trek that takes place every day we live.

Walking with Purpose

My children's first steps always involved goals that they were trying to achieve. Their mother or I stood in front of them with our arms outstretched, inviting them to come to us so we could catch them in our arms. Then we praised them for what they had just done, turned them around, and told them to go again, usually into the arms of the other parent who was waiting on the opposite side of the room. You get the picture. The point is that our walk always has an end in view.

Most of the time, we have an immediate purpose for where we are going. We go to work. We have goals and ends for which we are responsible in our sphere of employment. We take children to school, or we go to school. We go to the store. We take care of our daily needs and responsibilities. As we do all of these things, there are conscious and unconscious goals that we are aware of—or unaware of. However, everything is done with a specific task in mind.

Sometimes difficulties arise when we lose sight of—or do not know—our ultimate purpose. The immediate goal for my children was to walk. Ultimately, we taught them to walk so they could move through this world with the physical abilities they needed to survive and grow. We must know our ultimate purpose in life. If we are just trying to get through the day, meeting immediate goals and existing from one event to the next, then when something unexpectedly interrupts what we are doing, bringing conflict and turmoil with it, our response to it will come from an uninformed mind, will, or emotion. This will, in many instances, throw us into confusion, anger, rage, devaluation, depression, and, in some cases, despair.

There is a bigger picture here. Allowing the living God to reveal truth to us, let's consider the following verses taken from

Scripture. Instead of commenting on them individually, I am going to quote them all and then make a general observation.

"Therefore we also have as our ambition, whether at home or absent, to be pleasing to Him [Jesus Christ]" (2 Corinthians 5:9). "Whether, then, you eat or drink or whatever you do, do all to the glory of God" (2 Corinthians 10:31). "Whatever you do in word or deed, do all in the name of the Lord Jesus, giving thanks through Him to God the Father" (Colossians 3:17). "For you were formerly darkness, but now you are Light in the Lord; walk as children of Light (for the fruit of the Light consists in all goodness and righteousness and truth), ... always giving thanks for all things in the name of our Lord Jesus Christ to God, even the Father" (Ephesians 5:8–10, 20).

These are pretty definite directives. Our lives are to be seen as having purpose and meaning. We are not just strolling through life, helpless, hopeless, hapless, and directionless. Jesus Christ is to be given glory and thanks, and we are to be producing "goodness and righteousness and truth." This reflects the first question of the *Westminster Shorter Catechism*, which says: "What is the chief end of man? Man's chief end is to glorify God, and to enjoy Him forever" (*The Westminster Shorter Catechism*, Christian Education and Publications Study Material, Lawrenceville, GA, p. 3).

As we walk through this world, as you and I live our particular lives, we are able to meet whatever comes to challenge us by keeping our purpose before us. The drudgery of life is no longer the day-in, day-out struggle to keep our spirits high. Instead, we realize that in everything we do, every day we do it, there is the opportunity to give glory to God and enjoy life, because it actually counts for something. Despair can be countered with the truth that says, "Wait a minute. Even right now, the glory of God can be demonstrated by a change of attitude." Everything changes.

The apostle Paul says, "Not that I have already obtained it or have already become perfect, but I press on so that I may lay hold of that for which also I was laid hold of by Christ Jesus. Brethren, I do not regard myself as having laid hold of it yet; but one thing I do; forgetting what lies behind and reaching forward to what lies ahead, I press on toward the goal for the prize of the upward call of God in Christ Jesus" (Philippians 3:12–14).

We are always moving forward. We are always going upward. Our purpose is to "glorify God and to enjoy Him forever," to please Him, to ever, in all things, do what we do to bring honor to the name of Christ. As we continue this walk, this climb, we remind ourselves of who Christ is: "Buddha never claimed to be God. Moses never claimed to be Jehovah. Mohammed never claimed to be Allah. Yet Jesus Christ claimed to be the true and living God. Buddha simply said, "I am a teacher in search of the truth." Jesus said, "I am the Truth!" Confucius said, "I never claimed to be holy." Jesus said, "Who convicts me of sin?" Mohammed said, "Unless God throws his cloak of mercy over me, I have no hope." Jesus said, "Unless you believe in me, you will die in your sins" (*Nelson's Complete Book of Stories, Illustrations, and Quotes*, p. 480).

Jesus Christ and His glory are what we live for. He is God! He is the sinless sacrifice who takes away all our sins. He is truth. Knowing Him and making Him known is our high calling. In everything we do, we can glorify Him. Whether we are laboring at our jobs, taking our children to school and to their many activities, washing dishes, or taking out the garbage—whatever it is, in whatever capacity we are walking through the day—we can give glory to Christ Jesus. We walk with purpose!

Walking with God

There is not a more interesting or captivating verse in the Bible than Genesis 5:24: "Enoch walked with God; and he was not for God took him." I am not sure that I understand all that this implies. However, it does take me back to Genesis 3. Before Adam and Eve disobeyed God, there appeared to be a sweet, daily, continuous communion between our first parents and their Creator. Then, when they chose to rebel, Adam and Eve "heard the sound of the LORD God walking in the garden in the cool of the day" and "hid themselves from the presence of the LORD God among the trees of the garden" (Genesis 3:8). What seems to have been an enjoyable, loving walk with God during the day has turned into a time of separation and fear.

We need to return to whatever characterized Enoch and his constant movement through life. God was always there, providing Enoch with His presence, power, comfort, wisdom, and anything else that was needed. This is what companionship, walking with God, means. It is the most glorious reality that an individual can experience in this life. Think of it! God, who created everything and sent His Son to die in order to remove the guilt of sin, desires to walk with us, even as we take each step through a world filled with wickedness and evil that seek every opportunity to crush us. We are encouraged to "walk by the Spirit," even as we are to "live by the Spirit" (Galatians 5:25). As we do this, our lives begin to take on true worth and value.

Let me try to give you a picture of how this can work in your life. I have been through a very personal struggle over the past five or six years. It is one of those things that you think will never happen to you, but it does. In the midst of it, great friends recommended different things for me to read. One of the books I read got me thinking about this whole idea of walking with God

5

and personalizing it in my life. The germ of what I am going to tell you here came from that book. I really don't remember the name of the book, and it is not in my possession at this time. I do remember that it was a female author. Because of what I read, I began to practice something in my life that I still practice today, and it has been a catalyst in helping me consciously seek to walk with God.

There are times during the day when I literally stop what I am doing. I see myself leaning back and resting in the arms of Christ, my Savior, and putting my weight upon His chest, much in the same way that the apostle John is reported to have done at the Lord's Supper in John 13:23. I see Jesus smile and hear Him say, "George, man of God, I love you. I am delighted in you. You are mine. Nothing and no one can touch You." Then I picture Christ standing beside me, His arm intertwined with mine. He is there, ready to hold me up when I fall or stumble. I visualize Him standing in front of me, taking my hand and leading me through the circumstances and situations of life. I know He is over me, praying for me, presenting me to the Father, interceding on my behalf (Hebrews 7:25), always seeking my good and offering forgiveness for my sins and strength to raise me up when I am tempted and sin wins out. Amazingly, I know Christ is also living within me in the person of the Holy Spirit to give me grace and power to live in Christlikeness. As I picture all of this, I am praying, asking that the reality of what I am visualizing will overwhelm me and direct my steps.

I go through this mental exercise often throughout the day, longing to keep before me the immeasurable truth that I am walking with God and God is walking with me. It is when I forget this that my heart grows weary and I am ready to faint. I am not alone in this world. I have a King, a Savior, a Comforter, a Guide, and a Power Source who is ever with me and in me.

Walking Circumspectly

Imagine going into a windowless room filled with furniture, where all the lights are turned out—not only in that room but in all the adjacent rooms—closing your eyes, and trying to walk around the space without bumping into walls, chairs, tables, and other obstacles. It is an interesting exercise and a painful one. You quickly learn how difficult it would be to live as a person without physical sight. I have actually tried this, and after only seconds have walked into hard objects that hurt. In a panic, I looked for the nearest light switch. We all want to see where we are going.

This is true not only in a physical sense but in the spiritual sense. Just as we need to see where we are going to avoid potholes, curbs, cliffs, cars, mud, and things that might harm us physically, we need to see what will hurt us spiritually, leading us into depression and despair, causing us needless pain and suffering, and wounding our hearts. We cannot walk through this life with our spiritual eyes closed. We must look about and be aware of all that would seek to trip us up and destroy us. Nobody I know seems to have liked the movie *Green Lantern* with Ryan Reynolds. I guess I am a sucker for such superhero films. In the movie, we are told Green Lantern's oath, what he is sworn to uphold with his very life: "In brightest day, in darkest night, no evil shall escape my sight. Let those who worship evil's might, beware my power, Green Lantern's light." How cool is this?

All of us need to recognize the evil that we face on a daily basis. We must walk circumspectly! There are three enemies that face us, seeking to wreak havoc in our lives. God calls them the world, the flesh, and the Devil. Regardless of whether or not we believe in a personal devil, the effects of bad things happening to us are more than evident in this life. The pleasures of this world, the pride that creeps into our thoughts and actions continuously, and the things that bring sadness and conflict are lurking around every corner.

The Green Lantern said, "Beware my power, Green Lantern's light!" We are also given light: the Light of the world in the very person of Jesus Christ. "I am the light of the world; he who follows Me shall not walk in darkness, but shall have the light of life" (John 8:12). It is this light that gives life to every individual who receives Him (John 1:4, 9, 12). There is life here! There is light! Christ in all His glory causes people to see where they are going, what might loom as devastating obstructions in their lives, and how they can overcome whatever they face. We are told to "walk as children of light" (Ephesians 5:8), and "if we walk in the light, as He Himself is in the light, we have fellowship with one another, and the blood of Jesus His Son cleanses us from all sin" (1 John1:7).

Darkness only produces destruction. Light shows us the way. We can walk without falling into a pit. Actually, "all things become visible when they are exposed by light" (Ephesians 5:13). We are to be "careful" in the way we walk, "not as unwise men but as wise" (Ephesians 5:15). The darkness comes from inside. There may be outside influences, but these things cause us to stumble and fall: "being filled with unrighteousness [wrong choices and evil decisions], greed, evil; full of envy, murder [personal destruction of character], strife, deceit, malice, gossips, slanderers, haters of God, insolent, arrogant, boastful, inventors of evil, disobedient to parents, without understanding, unloving, unmerciful" (Romans 1:29–31 *Amplified Bible*). This is true darkness, and only the light that comes from the Spirit of Christ can replace it with "love, joy, peace, patience, kindness, goodness, faithfulness, gentleness, self-control" (Galatians 5:22–23). What a contrast!

Walk circumspectly. It is the only way to go!

Walk with Wisdom

As you can tell, all of these actions in our walk are bound together. In doing one, you will be doing the others. This is true of walking in wisdom. Of course, the wisdom we are speaking about is God's wisdom. There is a wisdom "which comes down from above" (James 3:15). At the same time, there is also a wisdom that comes from the root of "bitter jealousy and selfish ambition," which are "earthly, natural, demonic" (James 3:15). Where "jealousy and selfish ambition exist, there is disorder and every evil thing" (James 3:16).

What we want to do is to see things as God sees them. Vance Havner makes this astute observation: "If I could stand for five minutes at His vantage point and see the entire scheme of things as He sees it, how absurd would be my dreads, how ridiculous my fears and tears" (Vance Havner, *Consider Jesus* [Grand Rapids, Mich.: Baker Book House, 1987], 50). Our ability to be able to say with Paul, "For I have learned to be content in whatever circumstance I am" (Philippians 4:11), comes from the conviction that I don't look at the situation, but I look to almighty God, who is in control of all things. This is wisdom. It is a wisdom that causes us to understand, to know how—in light of seeing things from God's vantage point—we can respond with a proper attitude.

Of course, God's view of our lives and all that is going on around us is revealed in His will and mind, as set forth in His written Word. We become students of the Word in order to walk as those who possess proper eyeglasses to see what looms before us. God gives us many directives to help us in our walk.

For illustrative purposes, let's look at one of the things we are told by a wise God to do: "Do not fret or have any anxiety about anything, but in every circumstance and in everything, by prayer

9

and petition [definite requests], with thanksgiving, continue to make your wants known to God" (Philippians 4:6 *AB*). Fretting and living in fear are things we tend to do on a daily basis. How do we live in peace and calmness? What does worrying do? Does it make us strong? Does it change the circumstances, situations, or relationships we are facing? Of course not! Being in this frame of mind actually spoils lives and leads to inactivity or compulsive action that often brings even greater despair.

We want to walk with wisdom! We want to see things as God sees them. What do we do? We set aside anxiety in the midst of everything and instead pour out our hearts to God. We present every concern to Him. As we pray, we offer thanksgiving, which implies humility and submission to God's rule, knowing that His will is always best, good, right, and just. There must be thanksgiving for past favors, present blessings, and firmly grounded assurances for the future. This is to be done "before God," in His presence, knowing that He is almighty and has declared His unfailing love for us by giving His Son to die on the cross.

What is the result of doing this? Philippians 4:7 (AB) is so sweet: "And God's peace [shall be yours, that tranquil state of a soul assured of its salvation through Christ, and so fearing nothing from God and being content with its earthly lot of whatever sort that is, that peace] which transcends all understanding shall garrison and mount guard over your hearts and minds in Christ Jesus."

This is what God is going to do. He is going to take His peace, the fixed assurance that God is in control of everything, and let it act as a guard or sentinel at the door of our thoughts, our feelings, and our choices. This peace will prevent worry from corroding our hearts—which is the mainspring of life (Proverbs 4:23) and the root of thought (Romans 1:21), will (1 Corinthians 7:37), and reason—and from entering the thought life. In effect, this peace will place us "in Christ Jesus," from which no one can dislodge us. This is God's wisdom! May it be our companion as we walk through this world.

Chapter 2

Running

I used to run on a daily basis. My distance was usually three miles, five or six times a week. Then my feet started giving me trouble, so I switched from running to the elliptical machine. Recently, I decided I would start running again. Even through I had done the elliptical at a fast pace for forty to forty-five minutes, I knew that to start running I was going to have to work myself back into it and strengthen certain muscles that I had not used in a long time. Walking and running are different. This is not only true from a physical perspective; it is also true spiritually. As we live each day, we need to have the mind-set of walking and running.

Running with the Prize Set before Us

During this short span that makes up our personal timeline, we should not be running blindly. This race, like any other race, has a prize to be won. When we wake up in the morning, knowing that this might be our last day on earth, the prize of life is to be ever before us. We are told in 1 Corinthians 9:24 (*AB*), "Do you not know that in a race all the runners compete but [only] one receives the prize? So run [your race] that you may lay hold [of the prize] and make it yours." There is a prize! It is a present prize and a future prize. In the present, it consists of the blessing of being "in Christ" and having His Spirit living in us. The future prize is our eternal glory, reigning with Christ Jesus.

When we are running with our eyes set on the prize, we are leaving behind what has already taken place. We are doing what the apostle Paul said he was doing, acknowledging that we are always in the race. "Not that I have now attained [this ideal], or have already been made perfect, but I press on to lay hold of (grasp) and make my own, that for which Christ Jesus (the Messiah) has laid hold of me and make me His own [yet]; but one thing I do [it is my one aspiration]: forgetting what lies behind and straining forward to what lies ahead, I press on toward the goal to win the [supremely and heavenly] prize to which God in Christ Jesus is calling us upward" (Philippians 3:12–14 *AB*).

Here the runner, the athlete, is straining to reach the prize God has set before him or her. Every day the race is on. Runners set aside what happened the day before and now live life in a disciplined and goal-oriented manner, with meaning and purpose. They know that they are moving toward the likeness of Jesus Christ here and now and toward eternal glory in the future. Every obstacle gives way to the runner's determination to finish the race. Paul's glorious affirmation should be the motto of one's life: "For to me, to live is Christ and to die is gain" (Philippians 1:21).

Running with Endurance

I have never run in a marathon, but I do remember the day I decided to run from the house to the soccer field where my son was playing. I had been upping my miles each week, and I was feeling good and stronger than I had ever felt. I believe the field was a good ten miles away and some hills were involved.

I almost died! I didn't run the whole way. Some walking accompanied the running, and there might even have been some crawling. I can't (or actually don't want to) remember. Anyway, you get the point. Running in this life is not a hundred-meter dash. It is a marathon. It starts the minute we come into this world and lasts until the last breath that comes from our mouths. The race is difficult and filled with all kinds of traps, pits, holes, and messy things. We have to keep at it. Life requires endurance. Running in this life means that I do not give up.

I hope you know by now that my purpose is never to give you just my opinion on something. I always intend to present truth. The only way to find truth or wisdom for life is through that which is revealed to finite man by the personal, infinite God in His written Word. It is God who tells us, "By your endurance you will gain your lives (souls)" (Luke 21:9). The idea here is one of "steadfastness" and "patient endurance" (W. E. Vine, *Vine's Expository Dictionary of Biblical Word* [Nashville: Thomas Nelson Publishers, 1985], 200).

As we walk, we are also running in a race that calls for great exertion and requires us to keep going without stopping. Jesus Christ tells us, "You will be hated by all because of My name, but it is the one who has endured to the end who will be saved (Matthew 10:22). Again, Jesus said, "But the one who endures to the end, he will be saved" (Matthew 24:13). It is "to the end" that we must go. Don't stop!

In more than one instance, as God speaks about this, the concept of endurance carries with it the idea of multiple trials, afflictions, difficulties, and temptations. James declared, "Consider it all joy, my brethren, when you encounter various trials [which includes the concept of temptations], knowing that the testing of your faith produces endurance. And let endurance have its perfect result, so that you may be perfect and complete, lacking in nothing" (James 1:2–4). Faith, which we will discuss later, is born in the midst of all kinds of discouraging circumstances and situations. This lead us to the endurance we must have and, in turn, makes us whole, missing nothing that we need in this life. In fact, not only are we to consider this process "all joy," but we are to "exult in our tribulations, knowing that tribulation brings about perseverance (endurance); and perseverance, proven character" (Romans 5:3-4a). All of this understanding comes from "considering" and "knowing." It has nothing to do with what we might be feeling in the midst of trials and tribulations. We simply run. And we endure, because we know what is true about life.

The endurance with which we are to run has a relationship to the prize we have already spoken about. Hebrews 10:36 declares, "For you have need of endurance, so that when you have done the will of God, you may receive what was promised." What has God promised? He has promised to give "to those who by perseverance in doing good ... glory and honor and immortality, eternal life" (Romans 2:7). There is a purpose and a goal in our endurance. We are to keep going in this life, knowing it is God's will for our lives and drawing upon His power to finish the race.

Running to Something and Running Away from Something

We already know that we are running to gain a prize, but it must also be noted that we should be running away from certain other things too. The apostle Paul was speaking to his son in the faith, Timothy, who was serving as a young, fledgling minister, about the "love of money" (1 Timothy 6:10). The exhortation is to "flee from these things," to run away from the very things that are "the root of all evils." This—and the cravings that come with it—has led some astray and caused them to wander "from the faith" and pierce "themselves through with many acute [mental] pangs" (1

Timothy 6:10 *AB*). We are not to be consumed with pleasures, money, happiness, cars, homes, bank accounts, power, position, or any of those things that lay hold of the heart. Actually, we are to be actively fleeing from them.

As we run away from things that will certainly destroy us, we pursue that which will provide us with life, here and in the ages to come. Wise instruction continued for young Timothy: "But as for you, O man of God, flee from all these things; aim at and pursue righteousness (right standing with God and true goodness), godliness (which is the loving fear of God and being Christlike), faith, love, steadfastness (patience), and gentleness of heart" (1 Timothy 6:11 *AB*). How great would it be if this occupied our minds and our endeavors each day? Think about it: we rise up, and our determined purpose is to pursue righteousness, godliness, faith, love, steadfastness, and gentleness of heart. No matter what is happening around us circumstances, situations, or difficult relationships—they are secondary to what we are focusing our thoughts and feelings on.

We want to see godly character developed in our lives. We want to affect others positively and see lives changed. Worry, depression, and discouragement don't plague us, because righteousness, godliness, faith, love, steadfastness, and gentleness of heart have become our aim. Other concerns reign in our minds. Our particular circumstances do not control us, but the character we are displaying does. We are seeking to pursue our high calling in Christ Jesus. Such pursuit radically changes us.

How many times have the everyday twists and turns of life brought destruction to our calmness and peace? Such things don't have to be a catastrophe. Actually, it's often the little things that set us off. We get up late because the alarm didn't go off, which makes us late for work or getting the kids to school. There's an accident as we are going to an appointment, and we are stuck in traffic. Our car has a flat tire. Someone forgets his or her homework. Everyone around us has expectations of us: our spouse, children, relatives, friends, and employers. In the midst of all our difficulties, our personal pride, demands, wants, and wishes come to the forefront and tend to destroy our relationships and ourselves.

What a difference it would make if, in the midst of it all, we were pursuing those character qualities that shift our attention off of ourselves and onto others and their needs. We need to run away from pride, selfishness, and all kinds of evil to pursue that which is good, edifying, and gloriously satisfying. We must ask ourselves: "What am I pursuing? What am I running after?"

Chapter 3

Fighting

One of the most difficult things I have ever done is to watch the first twenty-five minutes of the movie *Saving Private Ryan*. I have seen a lot of John Wayne movies depicting war, but they were never as real as this blood-bath of carnage and the ripping apart of bodies shown in this movie. In this scene, the US Marines are hitting the beaches and are being gunned down in the open by machine gun fire.

When the film came out, there was a man in the church I was pastoring, who had been in the infantry in World War II. He had been a scout for his platoon, always scouting ahead and meeting firsthand the battle to come. I asked him if he had gone to see *Saving Private Ryan*. He looked at me with eyes that were cold, hard, determined, and yet full of sadness and deep hurt and said, "No, I would not be able to watch it, and whatever they showed would never truly depict how utterly horrible it was."

I hope we all know that the life we live is a battlefield. Daily living is filled with firefights that have to do with people, situations, and circumstances that cause wounds and hurts and all kinds of disturbances in our lives. Not only are we affected by outward, physical fatigue, but often we suffer inward damage that is far worse. In the back of my Bible, I have taped a list of emotions. Most of them are negative emotions that well up inside of us and cause us and those closest to us great harm as we react to them. We may feel abandoned, afraid, alone, angry, annoyed, anxious, apprehensive, ashamed, betrayed, bitter, confused, critical, deceived, defensive, depressed, disappointed, discouraged, empty, fearful, foolish, frustrated, guilty, impatient, insecure, intimidated, jealous, judged, offended, hurt, overwhelmed, rejected, resentful, sad, small, stupid, threatened, unimportant, and worthless. We don't just battle over the way we receive and respond to things that invade our lives on a daily basis, but we also struggle with the inner passions that are being produced as the bombs and bullets go off around us.

Fighting with Proper Weapons

There is a great hymn of the church that is rarely sung anymore. Listen to its clarion call.

> Onward Christian soldiers, marching as to war
> With the cross of Jesus going on before;
> Christ the royal Master leads against the foe:
> Forward into battle, see, his banners go.
>
> At the sign of triumph Satan's heart doth flee;
> On then, Christian soldiers, on to victory:
> Hell's foundations quiver at the shout of praise;
> Brothers, lift your voices, loud your anthems raise.
>
> Like a mighty army moves the church of God;
> Brothers, we are treading where the saints have trod;
> We are not divided, all one body we,
> One in hope and doctrine, one in charity.

Crowns and thrones may perish, Kingdoms rise and wane,
But the church of Jesus constant will remain;
Gates of hell can never 'gainst that church prevail;
We have Christ's own promise, and that cannot fail.

Onward then, ye people, join our happy throng,
Blend with our your voices in the triumph song;
Glory, laud, and honor unto Christ the King:
This through countless ages men and angels sing.

Refrain

Onward, Christian soldiers, marching as to war,
With the cross of Jesus going on before.

—Trinity Hymnal: Revised Edition
(Atlanta: Great Commission Publications, 1990), 572

We are always ready to turn everything into a hospital when we are caring for people's hurts and wounds—not just for days and weeks but for months and years. The problem is that we do not acknowledge and recognize that life itself is a field of battle. We are involved in warfare every day. We do not have the luxury of holing up in a hospital ward. Every day we are called upon to fight. We must make our preparation each day as we rise up to fight against every foe that comes against us.

If we must fight every day in this life, how important is it for us to know what kind of weapons we need for this battle? Dumb question, huh? It is paramount! This is why the written Word of God is so important to our lives. There is a passage in Ephesians 6 that tells us what our weapons are in this fight. It begins by saying that our position is to be one in which we are "strong in the Lord and in the strength of His might" (v. 10). We approach our lives from the position of power. Our strength is in the Lord God

21

and His might, not our own. We fight from this vantage point. Everything rests on our knowledge of God and who He is—and the realization that He is our power source.

My potency comes from living in the reality of this understanding. I dress myself "in the full armor of God" (Ephesians 6:11). The weapons I have come from the knowledge and understanding of God and His armor. All of God's Word declares to us the character of God. One of the greatest documents of the Christian church, *The Westminster Confession of Faith*, gives us an exact summation of the nature of the God whom we are to carry into battle with us:

> There is but one only living and true God, who is infinite in being and perfection, a most pure spirit, invisible, without body, parts, or passions, immutable, immense, eternal, incomprehensible, almighty, most wise, most holy, most free, most absolute, working all things according to the counsel of his own immutable and most righteous will, for his own glory; most loving, gracious, merciful, long-suffering, abundant in goodness and truth, forgiving iniquity, transgression, and sin; the rewarder of them that diligently seek him; and withal most just and terrible in his judgments; hating all sin, and who will by no means clear the guilty. — G. I. Williamson, *The Westminster Confession of Faith for Study Classes, Second Edition* (New Jersey: Presbyterian and Reformed Publishing, 2004), 30

Pretty impressive! This is the God with whom we have the privilege of walking into the greatest of conflicts. No power is greater than the power we have.

In addition, we have particular pieces of armor to help us. We have a belt that we are to put around us, "having girded your loins with truth" (Ephesians 6:14). It is the *truth* that we are to put on.

We are to see things as God sees them. People and circumstances are seen in light of the reality of who God is, who man is, what trials and afflictions are for, who is in control of all things, and how we are to handle all situations as they come into our lives.

The "breastplate of righteousness" (6:14) is also part of our armor. Regardless of what is happening or going on around us, we continue to live a life of obedience to our great Lord and Savior, seeking to please Him in all things. As we are assailed by all kinds of destructive forces, we move forward, living as those who are followers of Christ, undaunted and unchecked.

Our feet are covered with "the preparation of the gospel of peace" (6:15). We walk around, carrying the "good news" that we have a Savior who has come into the world to make us right with a holy God. Jesus gave His life on the cross to pay for our sins and to remove our guilt. He gives us His perfect righteousness so that the living God is now our heavenly Father, and we are no longer His enemies but His sons and daughters. We have peace with God, and therefore we have peace inside and the ability to build peace with others. This is great power.

In fact, this peace, this calm confidence in knowing the living God and knowing that He is in control of all things, can replace our feelings of being abandoned, alone, angry, annoyed—and all those other negative emotions we mentioned before—with "love, patience, kindness, goodness, faithfulness, gentleness, self-control" (Galatians 5:22–23). What a weapon!

There is also a "shield of faith" (v. 16). The great, almighty God is the one we hold up as our hope, comfort, and strength, and as our sovereign King. We throw ourselves upon Him in blessed assurance that nothing can touch us or hurt us as long as we are holding on to Him. Even though we cannot see what is going to happen, we know who our God is, and we know how great His love is for us as we camp out at the foot of the cross. We fear nothing! We live by unwavering trust! We use our shield to "extinguish all the flaming arrows of the evil one" (v. 16).

Faith of our fathers! Living still
In spite of dungeon, fire, and sword
Oh how our hearts beat high with joy
When-e'er we hear God's glorious Word:

Our fathers, chained in prisons dark,
Were still in heart and conscience free;
And blest would be their children's fate
If they, like them, should die for thee:

Faith of our fathers! God's great pow'r
Shall draw all nations unto thee;
And through the truth that comes from God
His people shall indeed be free:

Faith of our fathers! We will love
Both friend and foe in all our strife,
And preach thee, too, as love knows how
By witness true and virtuous life:

Refrain

Faith of our fathers, holy faith!
We will be true to thee till death.

—Trinity Hymnal, 570

The armor of God that we have been given also has a "helmet of salvation" (v. 17). Everything pertaining to our relationship with the triune God of this universe, now and forevermore, is bound up in what we have, figuratively, sitting on our heads. Inherent in our helmet of salvation is the condition of being made right with God, being adopted as children of God, dying more to sin each day and living more unto righteousness, being kept in God's grace until the day we draw our last breath, and being brought into the presence of Christ for all eternity.

We also hold an offensive weapon, "the sword of the Spirit, which is the word of God" (v. 17). It is used to defeat false teaching and ideologies that come against us from the outside world. At the same time, our greatest battle is often in our own hearts involving our feelings, emotions, passions, responses, and desires. Here too this weapon gives us clarity and truth that we need to make wise choices. The great thing about the Word of God is that it "is alive and full of power [making it active, operative, energizing, and effective]; it is sharper than any two-edged sword, penetrating to the dividing line of the breath of life (soul) and [the immortal] spirit, and of joints and marrow [of the deepest parts of our nature], exposing and sifting and analyzing and judging the very thoughts and purposes of the heart" (Hebrews 4:12 *AB*). This sword works especially well on the inner man. We have been given the proper weapons. They are weapons that are "divinely powerful for the destruction of fortresses" (2 Corinthians 10:4). It is our responsibility to use them.

Fighting and Knowing Who Your Enemies Are

What are we fighting? Whom are we fighting? What or who has the potential to cause us the greatest harm and hurt? When we try to answer these questions, our tendency is to look to external forces or relationships that have done their damage in our lives. It would actually be easier to engage in warfare with outside entities that we can easily identify and take out. The reality is that these are not our enemies. Our greatest enemy lies within, and it causes us to respond to outside influences in wrong and destructive ways.

Let's look back at our first parents. The example of Adam and Eve is instructive as we attempt to understand our adversaries in this world. These two representatives of men and women lived in a garden. It was a wonderful place of peace, rest, fulfilling labor, innocence, purity, and glorious communion with the God of creation in whose image they had been made. God gave them only one command to keep: they were not to eat of the Tree of Knowledge of Good and Evil.

Then the enemy of God and man, the Devil, manifested as a serpent, came and tempted the image-bearers. Satan was the Enemy, the tempter of all mankind. He was even the one who sought to tempt Jesus Christ to worship him rather than the Father (Mark 1:3). Jesus said to those who did not understand His Word or believe in Him, "You are of your father the devil, and you want to do the desires of your father. He was a murderer from the beginning, and does not stand in the truth because there is no truth in him. Whenever he speaks a lie, he speaks from his own nature, for he is a liar and the father of lies" (John 8:44).

In Genesis 3, we read that Satan tempted Eve with the fruit of the Tree of Knowledge of Good and Evil. It was something pleasing to the eye, and it spoke to her desires. "When the woman saw that the tree was good for food, and that it was a delight to the eyes, and that the tree was desirable to make one wise, she took from the fruit and ate; and she gave also to her husband with her and he ate" (v. 6). In connection with this, the apostle John gave us a true picture of the world we live in: "For all that is in the world, the lust of the flesh and the lust of the eyes and the boastful pride of life, is not from the Father, but is from the world" (1 John 2:16). These descriptions demonstrate that our very natures were involved in the enticement of Satan upon the heart of Eve. The world and Satan are both our enemies.

However, public enemy number one is our own inward man, characterized by our thoughts, feelings, and choices. We should say no to Satan and the world. The problem is that the greatest battle comes from within. Satan initially attacked Eve's thought process. He wanted her to question the character of God and the words God had said to her. Satan got Eve to believe a lie and to act on that belief. First, she began to think a certain way: *God is afraid I will become as wise as He is. Why, I can become like God Himself! I won't die. He lied to me!* Then Eve saw the fruit as desirable, something she wanted, so she took it and ate it.

Making choices is all about truth! If we are not thinking accurately and truthfully about what is going on around us, we will act and feel in ways that are wrong and will lead to personal loss and ruin. All Satan did was get Eve to believe a lie about God's goodness, sovereignty, and uniqueness. Paul told the believers in the church at Corinth, "We are destroying speculations and every lofty thing raised up against the knowledge of God, and we are taking every thought captive to the obedience of Christ" (2 Corinthians 10:5).

The fight is real. Just before this, Paul had said, "For though we walk in the flesh, we do not war according to the flesh. For the weapons of our warfare are not of the flesh, but divinely powerful for the destruction of fortresses" (2 Corinthians 10:3–4). We have the very Spirit of God living within us to help us think according to God's Word and see things truthfully as He sees them. Then we can destroy those things that the world and Satan throw at us. We fully understand that "our struggle is not against flesh and blood, but against the rulers, against the powers, against the world forces of this darkness, against the spiritual forces of wickedness in the heavenly places" (Ephesians 6:12).

Every day, we are to present our very lives, understanding, abilities, talents, and wisdom as a "living and holy sacrifice, acceptable to God," knowing that this is the worship our heavenly Father deserves (Romans 12:1). In doing this, we are carrying out the imperative given to us: "And do not be conformed to this world, but be transformed by the renewing of your mind, that you may prove what the will of God is, that which is good and acceptable and perfect" (Romans 12:2).

Our minds are to be renewed. We are to think differently from the Devil, the world, and our own tendencies of the flesh. Thoughts must be taken prisoner, brought before the truth of God's Word, and changed on the basis of what God says is true, not as our enemies present things to us. Light dispels darkness. We are told over and over again that Jesus Christ is the Light of the World.

Our enemies are at work every day, every minute, influencing what we think, feel, and choose. The Devil, the world, and the flesh are actively seeking to cause us to see evil as good and good as evil. It is not just Satan who wants us to see God as a liar. Know the enemy! Prepare for battle! Do not sleep! Do not rest! Keep alert!

Fighting and Knowing What Is at Stake

There is always a danger in quoting long passages of Scripture, because the tendency of the reader is to skip over it and get to the body of what is being said. However, I believe that this portion is so important I am going to quote it anyway and hope that it will be read. Here is Romans 8:5–17, with my own emphasis added.

> Those who live as their human nature tells them to, have their *minds* controlled by what human nature wants. Those who live as the Spirit tells them to, have their *minds* controlled by what the Spirit wants. To

be controlled by human nature results in *death*; to be controlled by the Spirit results in *life* and *peace*. And so a person becomes an *enemy* of God when he is controlled by his human nature; for he does not obey God's law and in fact he cannot obey it. Those who obey their human nature cannot please God.

But you do not live as your human nature tells you to; instead, you live as the Spirit tells you to—if, in fact, God's Spirit lives in you. Whoever does not have the Spirit of Christ does not belong to him. But if Christ lives in you, the Spirit is *life* for you because you have been put right with God, even though your bodies are going to die because of sin. If the Spirit of God, who raised Jesus from the dead, lives in you, then he who raised Christ from death will also give *life* to your mortal bodies by the presence of His Spirit in you.

So then, my brothers, we have an obligation, but it is not to live as our human nature wants us to. For if you live according to your human nature, you are going to *die*; but if by the Spirit you put to death your sinful actions, you will *live*. Those who are led by God's Spirit are *God's sons*. For the Spirit that God has given to you does not make you *slaves* and cause you to be afraid; instead, the Spirit makes you *God's children*, and by the Spirit's power we cry out to God, "Father! My Father!" God's Spirit joins himself to our spirits to declare that we are *God's children*. Since we are his *children*, we will possess the blessings he keeps for his people, and we will also possess with Christ what God has kept for him, for if we share Christ's sufferings, we will also share his glory.

—*Good News Bible* (GNT),
(New York: American Bible Society, 1976), 210

What a picture of the battle we face and what will be gained or lost to us every day of our lives! Life is not a game. It is not a competition to see who can get the most toys, achieve the most success, attain the most power, or acquire the most happiness. It is about something far more important: minds controlled by God's Spirit or minds controlled by the flesh; peace or disorder; children or slaves. Most importantly, it is about life or death. The fight we are engaged in is about our very souls, here and now and for all eternity.

The focal point of the Romans passage quoted above is the constant clash between the Spirit of God and the flesh. The flesh, our human nature, is always opposed to the things of God and always seeks to enslave us to those things that are dark, selfish, wicked, prideful, and evil. What is labeled "the flesh" must be replaced with the Spirit of God. It is only by the Spirit of God that we can "put to death" those sinful actions that flow out of our nature. We must acknowledge this nature and realize that the only way we can become "God's children," His sons and daughters, is by embracing Christ and believing that he has the power to put His Spirit within us and make us "new creatures" in Christ (2 Corinthians 5:17). Then we are given the power and right to cry out to God: "Father! My Father!" There is a new spirit within us, and we can now do battle with the very things that seek to lead us to death and destruction.

As the day dawns, we rise up with the resurrected Christ living within us through the person of the Holy Spirit. We put on the armor of God and fight against every enemy we have—the Devil, the world, and the flesh—knowing that our minds and souls hang in the balance. We also know that we will be victorious. We will possess not only the blessings God has promised to His people but all that belongs to the unique Son of God. Our position is one of being "fellow heirs with Christ" (Romans 8:17, NASB).

Here is the secret. We must have the Spirit of Christ living within us. We cannot fight this battle, this spiritual, inward warfare, by ourselves. We need a power that is not our own. I include here a simple prayer for you to use. Pray it with sincerity of heart and mind, and Christ will invade your life to sit as King over all you are and have. Here is the prayer:

Lord Jesus, I believe You are the Son of God. Thank You for dying on the cross for sin. Please forgive my sins and give me the gift of eternal life. I cast myself upon You in total reliance and embrace You as my Lord and Savior. I want to serve You always. Give me the ability to trust You. Work faith and repentance into my heart and life. In Jesus' name I pray, amen.

Chapter 4

Trusting

Every morning, I am always the first one at the office. I walk in and flip on the first light switch in the hall, move to the second one and then the third one, open the door to my office, and flip on that light switch. I then go to my computer, open it up, see that it comes to my opening page, and begin my morning devotions. I always do this, expecting the lights to come on and my computer to be up and running. All of us live like this every day. We trust that the lights are going to come on and that our computers are going to work. When something goes wrong, it is out of the ordinary, and we immediately do what needs to be done to fix the problem.

There is a television program called *Revolution*. It has an interesting premise: all the power is off. There is no more electricity. Everything that used to run on power no longer works. The whole purpose of our heroes is to get the power back on. The question in this story is: *whom or what do we trust?* The answer the show puts forth is: *no one!* However, the focus of the drama is on the fact that the characters *must* trust each other.

This is the point. We have to trust *someone* or *something* in order to live in this world. If we don't, we cannot function. Trust is the basis of our lives. We have to trust that those in our lives are going to carry out their roles and responsibilities so that our own day proceeds decently and in order. Of course, this doesn't always work out, but we still have to proceed in this manner. Otherwise, the only thing left for us would be to crawl into a corner, remove ourselves from all contact with other people, and die alone in despair.

Trust is simply holding onto the conviction that something is so, even though I cannot see it. For instance, I am sitting in my house. I am trusting that I can get up from my chair, walk outside, and go to my car, which is parked in the driveway where I left it. I cannot see my car from my chair, but I trust that it will be in the exact place where I put it. I do not go through any mental exercise over it. I just live with this kind of trust in my life all the time.

However, just as the TV show *Revolution* points out, the things of this world that we trust in—even the people we are closest to—often prove to be false and untrustworthy. One evening I actually did get out of my chair at home, walk out the front door to go to my car—and it was gone. Gone! Someone had stolen the car right out of my driveway. My heart sank. I was in shock, stunned, bathed in unbelief. Nothing like this had ever happened to me. I stood there, incredulous, wondering: "What do I do now?" Trust had been destroyed.

Regarding the things and people of this world, we put our trust in them, knowing they will break that trust. Who or what, then, will never break that trust? I love the story that longtime pastor, John Bisango, tells about his daughter, Melodye Jan. When she was five years old, she asked her dad for a dollhouse. Reverend Bisango nodded and promised to build her one and then went back to reading his book. It wasn't long before he glanced out of the window and saw his daughter, her arms filled with dishes, toys, and dolls, making trip after trip until she had a great pile in the yard. John asked his wife what Melodye Jan was doing.

"Oh, you promised to build her a dollhouse, and she believes you," said his wife. "She's just getting ready for it."

"You would have thought I'd been hit by an atom bomb," Bisango said. "I threw aside that book, raced to the lumberyard for supplies, and quickly built that little girl a dollhouse. Now, why did I respond that way? Because I wanted to? No. Because she deserved it? No. I did it because her daddy had given his word, and she'd believed it and acted upon it. When I saw her faith, nothing could keep me from carrying out my word" (John Bisango, *The Power of Positive Praying* [Grand Rapids, Mich.: Zondervan, 1965], 24).

Trust comes down to taking someone at his word. Whose word can we fully trust? The only person we can completely trust is our Creator and Redeemer. He is the One who made the heavens and the earth, formed us in His own image, and sent Christ Jesus into this world to die in our place. He is trustworthy. Just as Melodye Jan trusted her earthly father, even though he actually failed in the trust department, we can trust our heavenly Father's Word every time. HE WILL NOT FAIL!

Trusting in the Lord

It is evident that the things or people we trust in will fail us. When we turn on the lights, they don't always work. Putting a key in the ignition of a car and turning it to the on position doesn't guarantee that it will start. Telling our loved ones to do something doesn't mean that they will always do it. Vows are broken. All of us have deceived and told lies. We fail each other. We are imperfect, and we live in an imperfect world. Still, we have to live by trust. There would be only despair and doom without it.

There is only one who is a sure and certain hope, an anchor for the soul. Over and over, we are told in God's written revelation that we are to trust in Him. He will not fail us. Here are just a few verses from the New King James Version that exhort us to trust in the Lord:

"Offer the sacrifices of righteousness, and put your trust in the LORD" (Psalm 4:5).

"Trust in Him at all times, you people: pour out your heart before Him; God is a refuge for us" (Psalm 62:8).

"Trust in the LORD, and do good; dwell in the land, and feed on His faithfulness" (Psalm 37:3).

"In the LORD I put my trust" (Psalm 11:1).

"Trust in the LORD with all your heart, and lean not on your own understanding; in all your ways acknowledge Him, and He shall direct your paths" (Proverbs 3:5–6).

"You will keep him in perfect peace, whose mind is stayed on You, because he trusts in You. Trust in the LORD forever, for in YAH, the LORD, is everlasting strength" (Isaiah 26:3–4)

"Though He slay me, yet will I trust in Him" (Job 13:15).

"And those who know Your name will put their trust in You: for You, LORD, have not forsaken those who seek You" (Psalm 9:10).

"But as for me, I trust in You, O LORD; I say, 'You are my God'" (Psalm 31:14).

"Yes, we had the sentence of death in ourselves, that we should not trust in ourselves but in God who raises the dead, who delivered us from this great death, and does deliver us; in whom we trust that He will still deliver us" (1 Corinthians 1:9–10).

"Command those who are rich in this present age not to be haughty, nor to trust in uncertain riches, but in the living God, who gives us richly all things to enjoy" (1 Timothy 6:17).

"Therefore humble yourselves under the mighty hand of God, that He may exalt you in due time, casting all your care upon Him, for He cares for you" (1 Peter 5:6–7).

"In whom [Christ] we have boldness and access with confidence through faith in Him" (Ephesians 3:12).

Over and over again, we are told to put our trust in the Lord, or we are shown what trusting in the Lord produces in our lives. We are not trusting in just anything. The object of our belief is none other than the Sovereign God who rules over all. We are trusting in His character, His power, His wisdom, His promises, His faithfulness, and His unfailing love. Consider God's overwhelming declarations about who He is, according to the *New American Standard Bible.*

"The LORD shall reign forever and ever" (Exodus 15:18).

"Know therefore today, and take it to heart, that the LORD, He is God in heaven above and on earth below; there is no other" (Deuteronomy 4:39).

"O LORD, the God of our fathers, are You not God in the heavens? And are You not ruler over all the kingdoms of the nations? Power and might are in Your hands so that no one can stand against You" (2 Chronicles 20:6).

"Because of you raging against Me, and because your arrogance has come to My ears, therefore, I will put My hook in your nose, and my bridle in your lips, and I will turn you back by the way which you came" (2 Kings 19:28).

"The LORD sat as King at the flood; yes, the LORD sits as King forever" (Psalm 47:2).

"Who is the King of glory? The LORD of hosts, He is the King of glory" (Psalm 24:10).

"For the LORD Most High is to be feared, a great King over all the earth" (Psalm 47:2).

"That they might know that You alone whose name is the LORD, are the Most High over all the earth" (Psalm 83:18).

"The LORD reigns, He is clothed with majesty; the LORD has clothed and girded Himself with strength; indeed, the world is firmly established, it will not be moved" (Psalm 93:1).

"Whatever the LORD pleases, He does, in heaven and earth, in the seas and in all the deeps" (Psalm 135:6).

"The King's heart is like channels of water in the hand of the LORD; He turns it wherever He wishes" (Proverbs 21:1).

"Behold the Lord God will come with might, with His arm ruling for Him. Behold His reward is with Him and His recompense before Him ... Do you not know? Have you not heard? Has it not been declared to you from the beginning? Have you not understood from the foundations of the earth? It is He who sits above the circle of the earth, and its inhabitants are like grasshoppers, who stretches out the heavens like a curtain, and spreads them out like a tent to dwell in. He it is who reduces rulers to nothing. Who makes the judges of the earth meaningless? Do you not know? Have you not heard? The Everlasting God, the LORD, the Creator of the ends of the earth does not become weary or tired. His understanding is inscrutable. He gives strength to the weary, and to him who lacks might He increases power" (Isaiah 40:10, 21–23, 27–29).

"Thus says the LORD, your Redeemer, and the One who formed you from the womb, 'I, the LORD, am the Marker of all things, stretching out the heavens by Myself, and spreading out the earth alone, causing the omens of boasters to fail, making fools out of diviners, causing wise men to draw back, and turning their knowledge into foolishness'" (Isaiah 44:24–25).

"Daniel answered and said, 'Let the name of God be blessed forever and ever, for wisdom and power belong to Him. And it is He who changes the times and the epochs; He removes Kings and establishes Kings; He gives wisdom to wise men, and knowledge to men of understanding. It is He who reveals the profound and hidden things; He knows what is in the darkness, and the light dwells with Him'" (Daniel 2:20–22).

"The Most High is ruler over the realm of mankind, and bestows it on whomever He wishes" (Daniel 4:25).

"For His dominion is an everlasting dominion, and His Kingdom endures from generation to generation, and all the inhabitants of the earth are accounted as nothing, but He does according to His will in the host of Heaven and among the inhabitants of earth; and no one can ward off His hand or say to Him, 'What have You done?'"(Daniel 4:34–35).

"Pilate therefore said to Him, 'So You are a king?' Jesus answered, 'You say correctly that I am a king. For this I have been born and for this I have come into the world, to bear witness to the truth. Who is of the truth hears My voice'" (John 18:37).

"Men of Israel, listen to these words: Jesus the Nazarene, a man attested to you by God with miracles and wonders and signs, which God performed through Him in your midst, just as you yourselves know—this Man, delivered up by the predetermined plan and foreknowledge of God, you nailed to a cross by the hands of godless men and put Him to death. And God raised Him up again, putting an end to the agony of death, since it was impossible for Him to be held in its power" (Acts 21:22–24).

"And we know that God causes all things to work together for good to those who love God, to those who are called according to His purpose" (Romans 8:28).

"For I am convinced that neither death, nor life, nor angels, nor principalities, nor things present, nor things to come, nor powers, nor height, nor depth, nor any other created thing, will be able to separate us from the love of God, which is in Christ Jesus our Lord" (Romans 8:38–39).

"Now to the King eternal, immortal, invisible, the only God, be honor and glory forever and ever. Amen" (1 Timothy 1:17).

"And I heard, as it were, the voice of a great multitude and as the sound of many waters and as the sound of mighty peals of thunder, saying, 'Hallelujah! For the Lord our God, the Almighty reigns'" (Revelation 19:6).

Okay, stop for just a minute! I know what you have done. You have skipped reading all of these verses and come to this paragraph to pick up reading the narrative of this book. I beg you to go back and actually read these powerful and wonderful verses that actually tell you who it is that you are being asked to put your hope in.

It is so important that we see this, hear this, understand this, and confidently rest in the "one only living and true God, who is infinite in being and perfection, a most true spirit, invisible, without body, parts, or passions, immutable, immense, eternal, incomprehensible, almighty, most wise, most holy, most free, most absolute, working all things according to the counsel of his own immutable and most righteous will, for his own glory; most loving, gracious, merciful, long-suffering, abundant in goodness, forgiving iniquity, transgression, and sin; the rewarder of them that diligently seek him; and withal most just and terrible in his judgments; hating all sin and who will by no means clear the guilty" (*The Westminster Confession of Faith* [Atlanta: Committee for Christian Education and Publications, 1990], 8–10).

This is the God of the Bible. This is the God who asks you and me to bet everything on Him. I'm all in! What about you?

I like reading books of the same genre as *The Lord of the Rings* by J. R. R. Tolkien. You can always find these kinds of books in the science fiction section of any major bookstore chain. I am not sure why they are in this place in a bookstore, because I really don't consider them to be science fiction. In my opinion, they are epic tales of heroes and courage, battles and conflicts both physical and spiritual, and loyalty and faithfulness. *The Blinding Knife* by Brent Weeks is such a book.

In this heroic tale, Gavin is a drifter of colors. Each color carries with it the power to destroy. The commander who serves Gavin says the following in regard to what Gavin does in an effort to rule and save his people: "You do this all the time. You've been doing this since the war. You save people without them even knowing it. You've stopped wars, you've sunk pirates, you've put down wights, you've killed brigand companies single-handed. All without bragging or even asking for thanks. You are He Who Fights Before Us indeed ... Thank you ... for all you've done that I don't know. For the prices you've paid that I can't understand. For doing what others couldn't or wouldn't. Thank you ... It is an honor to serve *you*, ... and serve we shall, blood and bone" (Brent Weeks, *The Blinding Knife* [New York: Orbit Hachette Book Group, 2012], 523).

The commander truly appreciated Gavin. But listen! We have an awesome God who is even more "He Who Fights Before Us!" He is the God who has created and made us. Not only is he our Maker, but He is our Redeemer. We too, with a clear understanding of who He is and what He has done, should declare, with all the conviction of our hearts and lives, that we will serve Him and trust Him, "blood and bone!" Blood and bone! Declare it with me. Put down this book and say it to Him: "Lord God, Savior of my soul, defender of my life, I will trust You, blood and bone!"

Trusting with All Your Heart

On more than one occasion during the day, I find myself quoting Proverbs 3:5–6 to myself: "Trust in the LORD with all your heart and do not lean on your own understanding. In all your ways acknowledge Him, and He will make your paths straight."

It seems that there are so many things that happen each day that challenge my ability to rest in the Lord God and His control over all things. I start thinking about my children or grandchildren and begin to fret about how they are doing and what is going on in their lives. Thoughts concerning my ministry come to my mind, and I wonder whether I am being faithful and effective in what I am doing. A phone call comes concerning a church member's health situation or discontent, and I immediately begin to wrestle with how to pray for that person, speak into his life, or actually confront him, if that's what is necessary. Reading something, I begin to think about relationships and circumstances that loom before my mind and heart.

You know how this works. The same thing happens to all of us. We can take this into our homes. Our children say or do something, and immediately we are confronted with a situation that requires us to say or do something to address what has happened. The same thing can happen with our spouses or other family members. Throughout the day, we deal with our thoughts and our own or others' actions, all of which require us to wrestle with doubts and fears and the gnawing feeling that we just can't trust life or even God.

It seems that all earthly fathers do a particular thing with their children. I did it with all three of mine, and it is with great joy that I see my sons and son-in-law doing it with my grandchildren. What is it? It is the act of fathers picking up their little sons or daughters and tossing them into the air. It doesn't matter whether they throw them up and catch them, swing them around by their feet, or flip them over. Every child I have ever seen in this free-flying circumstance laughs, screams with excitement, and seems to always respond by saying, "Do it again!" Children find themselves in all kinds of strange, precarious positions, and yet they are all in, sometimes laughing until they cry or lose their breath, all the time wanting to do it over and over again. Why? Because they completely trust in their fathers, who are right there in the midst of all the flying, summersaulting, and catching. It is actually one of the greatest illustrations of what it means to trust in the Lord with all one's heart.

The story is told of five-year-old Jessica who had become frightened of lightning and thunder. One evening, she was about to take a bath, when the lightning flashed outside and the thunder boomed. The lights in the bathroom flickered, and she immediately became frightened that the lights would go out and she would be in the dark. She asked her mother if she could sleep in her mother's room because of the storm.

As Jessica was getting ready to kiss her parents goodnight, she prayed: "Dear God, I hope it doesn't thunder, and I hope the lights don't go out." After a moment of silence, realizing that she was now in the presence of her mother and father, she continued, "But I thought it over, and you can do what you want. In Jesus' name, amen" (Michael P. Green, ed., *Illustrations for Biblical Preaching* [Grand Rapids, Mich.: Baker Book House, 1990], 133).

This is what it is like to trust with all your heart. A five-year-old girl exhibiting complete, childlike trust is a weighty reminder to the adults of this world of how feeble our faith often is. It is interesting that the first time the concept of "the heart" is mentioned in the Bible is in Genesis 6:5. Here, it is actually describing the exact opposite of trust: "Then the LORD saw that the wickedness of man was great on the earth, and that every intent of the thoughts of his heart was only evil continually." The Amplified Bible gives the full meaning and intent of what God is saying here by translating the original language in this manner: "And that every imagination and intention of all human thinking was only evil continually."

From the Bible's perspective, the heart is the core of who a person is. The heart refers to the mind, the emotions, and the will. However, the key to who a person is centers in how a person thinks. How a person thinks determines how he feels and what he chooses. Thus, man's thinking, being "only evil continually," leads to great wickedness.

If people are going to trust the Lord God with all of their hearts, they must have good, right, and great thoughts about who God is, as we have already seen. Trusting God with our whole heart does not begin with our emotions or our wills; it begins with what we think about God. This goes back to the verses we have already mentioned in the previous section.

At one point in my ministry, I was getting ready to preach on 1 Chronicles 29:10–20, which is a prayer of David to His Sovereign God. David gave us a great picture of what he thought of God. The title of my sermon was "The Nothing before the All." We are nothing as we stand in the presence of almighty God.

As I was working on this sermon, someone gave me an audio tape to listen to. The tape was of a large gathering of black pastors. One of those men present was Dr. S. M. Lockridge. He was asked to say a word of greeting to the audience. He rose and gave a spontaneous, electrifying description of the living God. I was so taken aback by it that I listened to it over and over again, transcribing his exact words. Before I preached my sermon, I used this statement as an opening illustration and actually played the tape in the large sanctuary that held three thousand people.

You can listen to this on www.youtube.com, or you can read it by going to the Internet and typing in "S. M. Lockridge quotes." I suggest that you listen to it. There is nothing like hearing this man speak from his heart, powerfully and forcefully and with such conviction. I actually wanted to put it here in my book but was prevented from doing so by the publisher, who was quite adamant about getting permission to use it, even though it appears that there are no copyright laws attached to it and no one else makes any reference to permission received from family members or any other source.

Be that as it may, let me tell you about the statement. It goes on for about six minutes. I understand that Dr. Lockridge used it in a Sunday morning sermon. The content of the statement is about the nature and character of Jesus Christ. The truth of what he said was so much a part of him that he could call it up any time he was asked to do so. This was what took place on the tape that I listened to. He began by saying, "The Bible says ...," and then he went through a litany of descriptive sentences concerning the person and work of Christ, followed by, "That's my King. I wonder, do you know Him?"

Going through the historical landscape of Christ's saving work, Lockridge refer to Christ as the Sovereign King, God's Son, the Savior, the one who is righteous, all-powerful, all-wise, and full of mercy, truth, and grace. At the end of each segment, he said, "Do you know Him?" After using all those magnificent, descriptive adjectives to portray the Lord Jesus, and before his final portion, he said, "I wish I could describe Him." Of course, what he had done was to give us the most overpowering, inspiring look into the nature and character of Christ that could be given outside of the very pages of Scripture.

What Lockridge really wanted us to know was that no one has the ability, in words, to adequately portray the one who is the King of kings and Lord of lords. It is a futile to say to anyone, "Here is an exhaustive representation of the one who is Holy God, the second person of the Trinity." And at the end of this personal, intimate, loving tribute to Jesus Christ, Lockridge said, "That's my King!," having just given great affirmation to the title.

45

As I have listened to this statement over and over again, and as I have read it numerous times, it is quite evident that Dr. Lockridge knew the triune God of the Bible. He knew his Savior and King, Jesus Christ. I am convinced that this knowledge was not just head knowledge but was a vital, life-changing heart commitment, which made a difference in how Lockridge lived his life. The choices he made were made to please his Savior. No matter what was going on in his life, I am certain that he would be able to cleave and hold on to such a King and draw strength and comfort from such a loving ruler. The final statement in Lockridge's testimony was this: "Pilate couldn't find any fault with Him. The witnesses couldn't get their testimonies to agree. Herod couldn't kill Him; death couldn't handle Him; and the grave couldn't hold Him."

What about you and me? What do we think about the character of God? When we talk about trusting with all of our hearts, are we talking about the nature of the object we are trusting in? If our God is the One that Dr. Lockridge referred to, the One revealed in God's written Word and in the living Word, Jesus Christ, then our thoughts concerning Him will lead to an assured love and confidence in Him, and we will make life choices that honor and please the King. We will laugh and rejoice as He tosses us around in the air, knowing who He is and that His presence assures us of protection and safety. We too will be able to say, "Do it again!"

Trusting When It Appears There Is Nothing to Trust In

We are very emotional people. We feel things whether we want to admit it or not. Things happen to us that cause us to wonder, to question, to fear, to lose hope, and to imagine that everything is crashing in around us. There doesn't seem to be any immediate fix for the dilemma we are facing. Often, it is in these moments that we are told to "trust in God," but the current obstacles appear to be too great to overcome, and we really don't see or feel God in the midst of them. So, what do we do?

It is important that we stop and think. The key is not in how we feel but in what we know. Truth must overcome impressions, imaginations, hunches, experiences, appearances, intuitions, feelings, and emotions. Of course, this will only be true if we believe what God has said to us in His written revelation. If we have the authentic, authoritative Word of God, from God's very mouth, then, in the midst of whatever is going on, we can go to that Word and stand firm on what it says and meet any adversity in life.

We want to be able to see and know what is going to happen: how something is going to turn out, whether the sickness is going to lead to health or death, whether the loss of a job will be answered by an even better job or great suffering, whether the fight will lead to reconciliation or divorce, and so on. However, the whole point of living by faith, or trust, is that we hold onto the character of God and what He has promised, even without being able to see the outcome of a particular situation, "for we walk by faith, not by sight" (2 Corinthians 5:7).

I would direct you to that great New Testament chapter that addresses the whole subject of trust: Hebrews 11. *Trust* is actually the best synonym for *faith*, because it carries with it the concept of commitment and certainty, which are the key elements of faith. As we have already made clear, we are not talking about some blind faith but a commitment to and certainty in the very person of the triune God of the Scriptures. We are never left alone or in a place without hope, as long as we do not allow feelings and circumstances to rule in our lives. We must allow objective truth, not subjective pressure, to direct our paths.

Hebrews 11 begins with a great definition of the faith, the trust, that all of us are to exemplify. Let me quote it to you from the Amplified Bible: "Now faith is the assurance (the confirmation, the title deed) of the things [we] hope for, being the proof of things [we] do not see and the conviction of their reality [faith perceiving as real fact what is not revealed to the senses]. For by [faith—trust and holy fervor born of faith] the men of old had divine testimony borne to them and obtained a good report. By faith we understand that the worlds [during the successive ages] were framed (fashioned, put in order, and equipped for their intended purpose) by the word of God, so that what we see was not made out of things which are visible" (Hebrews 11:1–3). The rest of the chapter focuses on the people of God who lived by such faith.

If we read Genesis 22, we see that God brought to Abraham one of the greatest trials anyone could ever face. He had been promised God's covenantal love, multiplication of his seed to make him the father of a multitude of nations, and a land flowing with milk and honey (Genesis 17). All of this would come through his promised heir, Isaac. In this passage, God told Abraham to take Isaac, go up on the mountain, and sacrifice his promised son to God. You think things are tough in your life? You think that things are unfair, that certain things shouldn't happen to you? You think you are getting the raw end of things? You think there is no hope?

God told Abraham, "Take now your son, your only son [that is, the son who was connected to the covenant promise God had given him], whom you love, Isaac, and go to the land of Moriah, and offer him there as a burnt offering on one of the mountains of which I will tell you" (Genesis 22:2). There is no indication that Abraham argued with God, declared the unfairness of this demand, or pleaded with God not to do this. It simply says, "So

Abraham rose early in the morning and saddled his donkey, and took two of his young men with him and Isaac his son; and he split wood for the burnt offering, and arose and went to the place of which God had told him" (Genesis 22:3). Amazing!

Immediately, the question arises: "How could Abraham do this?" or maybe "*Why* did Abraham do this?" In Hebrews 11, the very passage where the concept of faith is treated and defined, the answer to our questions is given: "By faith, Abraham, when he was tested, offered up Isaac, and he who had received the promises was offering up his only begotten son; it was he to whom it was said, 'in Isaac your descendants shall be called.' He considered that God is able to raise people even from the dead, from which he also received him back as a type" (Hebrews 11:17–19).

Abraham did not know that God was going to provide a lamb caught in the bushes as a substitute for Isaac, but he knew the character of his God, the one who had made a promise to him, and he believed that his God had the power to perform a mighty miracle, if need be, to keep His promise. This is how trust operates.

Elisha, the prophet of God, was helping the king of Israel protect himself against the king of Aram. Every time the king of Aram attempted to come upon the king of Israel and his army, Elisha warned Israel. It got so bad that the king of Aram thought someone from his own camp had to be a traitor. Then one of his men told him, "No, my lord, O King; but Elisha, the prophet who is in Israel, tells the King of Israel the words that you speak in your bedroom" (2 Kings 6:12). So they sought to find Elisha and kill him. When they located Elisha, the King of Aram sent a great army after him. Elisha's servant went out in the morning and saw a great army surrounding the city.

This is how many of us feel as we live in this world. We are surrounded by the Enemy, and there appears to be no help and no hope. Over the past six years, I have experienced the greatest loss of my life, mainly family and friends. Every day I am plagued with a sense of hurt and sorrow that I must fight against, and oftentimes I have the nagging feeling of being alone. Sometimes I struggle even to get out of bed in the morning to pursue what God has called me to do. In the midst of this, I often think about Elisha and his servant. The servant rushed back to tell God's prophet about the impending doom they faced, and in great despair he cried out, "Alas, my master! What shall we do?" (2 Kings 6:15). This is a question that often gnaws at my own heart. "What shall I do?"

The narrative in 2 Kings says that Elisha prayed. He prayed that the Lord God would "open his [the servant's] eyes that he may see" (2 Kings 6:17). Elisha wanted the servant to see what Elisha believed and knew with a certain and sure trust. Elisha did not physically see what he wanted his servant to see. However, he wanted trust to be born in his servant, so he asked God to actually let the servant see what Elisha knew and trusted to be so. The next part of the scene is what I hold on to at all times: "And the LORD opened the servant's eyes [spiritual eyes] and he saw; and behold, the mountain was full of horses and chariots of fire all around Elisha."

How about that? There were "horses and chariots of fire" on every side to protect and provide for Elisha and his servant. Our faith does not come from what we see with our physical eyes; it comes from what we know. Elisha knew! The servant did not see what was there because he did not trust. Trust is based on God's promises to us.

Psalm 91:7, 10 says, "A thousand may fall at your side and ten thousand at your right hand, but it shall not approach you … No evil will befall, nor will any plague come near your tent." "Had it not been the LORD who was on our side … they would have swallowed us alive" (Psalm 124:1, 3). "As the mountains surrounded Jerusalem, so the LORD surrounds His people" (Psalm 125:2).

"Do you not know? Have you not heard? The Everlasting God, the LORD, the Creator of the ends of the earth does not become weary or tired. His understanding is inscrutable. He gives strength to the weary, and to him who lacks might he increases power. Though youths grow weary and tired, and vigorous young men stumble badly, yet those who wait for the LORD will gain new strength; they will mount up with wings like eagles, they will run and not get tired, they will walk and not become weary" (Isaiah 40:28–31). "Do not fear, for I am with you; do not anxiously look about you, for I am your God. I will strengthen you, surely I will help you, surely I will uphold you with My righteous right hand" (Isaiah 41:10).

Our struggles always seem to center around things that we consider bad and unjust. They revolve around circumstances that we don't think we or other people deserve. As we are confronted with difficult situations, turns of events, and broken relationships, our trust dissipates, and in many cases, self-pity and depression overtake us.

The prophet Habakkuk felt the same way. In fact, he actually entered into a conversation with God in the book of Habakkuk. Because of the sins of God's people, God was going to send a foreign nation to punish them. Habakkuk wanted to know how long this oppression would last and when it would come. The answer God gave to him was not the one he wanted to hear. God informed Habakkuk that the enemies would certainly come and that God would not tell His prophet how long the situation would last.

However, God did tell Habakkuk that He would eventually deliver His people, but not necessarily in Habakkuk's lifetime.

Habakkuk responded, "Though the fig tree should not bloom and there be no fruit on the vines, though the yield of the olive should fail and the fields produce no food, though the flock should be cut off from the fold and there be no cattle in the stalls, yet *I will exult in the LORD, I will rejoice in the God of my salvation.* The Lord GOD is my strength, and He has made my feet like hinds' feet, and makes me walk on high places" (Habakkuk 3:17–19, emphasis mine).

This is the whole point and purpose of trust. It is what we do when we can't see and don't understand. Almighty God is not obligated to explain anything to us. We are responsible to trust Him, His character, His nature, His covenant-keeping relationship with us, and His declaration of unconditional, sacrificial love, as demonstrated by Christ's death on the cross—*no matter what*!

As I write this section of this book, the horrific tragedy of Newtown, Connecticut, has just taken place. Twenty elementary-age school children have been needlessly slaughtered, along with faithful teachers and a principal. Since my subject is "trust" and not "God's sovereignty" or "the fallenness of this world" or "evil's origin," I will only say that the first three chapters of the book of Romans are a sober commentary on what took place on December 14, 2012. Paul made it very clear that because man has "exchanged the truth of God for a lie, and worshiped and served the creature rather than the Creator," God has given mankind "over to a depraved mind," which has caused His creations to be *"filled with all* unrighteousness, wickedness, greed, evil; full of envy, murder" (Romans 1:24, 28–29, emphasis mine). It is right here, at this point of irreconcilable horror and terror, that our hearts must dig into the great character and complete faithfulness of God, the Father of our Lord Jesus Christ, and *trust*!

It seems that we have a great aversion to the past, especially the history of the church. I remember preaching at a large, suburban church. After the worship service, I had lunch with the pastoral search committee. They were appreciative of my message, but they were very concerned that I had used too many illustrations from the past and not enough "contemporary" stories to speak to present-day audiences. I hope that the stories of how God has worked in the past in the lives of His people never grow old, that they will teach us at all times how we are to live in every age as the people of God.

Martin Luther lived at a time when everything was in turmoil. Luther had grown up listening to his mother sing. Music was a great part of his life. When the Protestant Reformation began, Luther was determined to restore worship to the German church. Luther's most famous hymn declared the need for the church to put its trust in the living God, no matter the cost. "A Mighty Fortress Is Our God" was not just a song of worship, but it was a song to call God's people to battle, to arms, and to stand firm in the midst of every opposition, even the Devil himself. This hymn is based on Psalm 46. In difficulty and danger, Luther often resorted to this song, saying to his associate, "Come, Philipp, let us sing the 46th Psalm" (Robert J. Morgan, *Then Sings My Soul*, p. 15). Here are the words to this great hymn. If you know the tune, don't just read it; I invite you to sing it.

> A mighty fortress is our God, a bulwark never failing;
> Our helper he amid the flood of mortal ills prevailing.
> For still our ancient foe doth seek to work us woe;
> His craft and pow'r are great; and armed with cruel hate,
> On earth is not his equal.
>
> Did we in our own strength confide, our striving
>   would be losing;
> Were not the right man on our side, the man of
>   God's own choosing.

Dost ask who that may be? Christ Jesus it is he,
Lord Sabaoth his name, from age to age the same;
And he must win the battle.

And though this world, with devils filled, should
        threaten to undo us,
We will not fear, for God hath willed his truth to
        triumph through us.
The prince of darkness grim, we tremble not for him;
His rage we can endure, for lo! his doom is sure;
One little word shall fell him.

That Word above all earthly pow'rs, no thanks to
        them abideth;
The Spirit and the gifts are ours through him who
        with us sideth.
Let goods and kindred go, this mortal life also;
The body they may kill; God's truth abideth still;
His kingdom is forever.

-Trinity Hymnal, 92

Trust never ceases. In the midst of all dangers—even the threats from our great Enemy—we stand. According to the last verse of Luther's hymn, *we win!* Those who are members of the kingdom of God *win!*

Many of us have probably never heard of Horatio G. Spafford. He was an attorney during the time of the great Chicago fire in 1871. He had invested a large some of money in real estate and had lost a fortune. At this time, his only son, age four, succumbed to scarlet fever. Yet, even in the midst of these losses, he poured himself into helping rebuild the city. In November of 1873, he decided to go on holiday with his wife and four daughters to Europe. Horatio had a very close relationship with evangelist D.

L. Moody and Ira Sankey, who led the singing during Moody's evangelistic campaigns. Spafford was going to go to London for Moody's meetings and then enjoy a vacation with his family.

An urgent matter detained Horatio in New York, so he decided to send his wife, Anna, and their daughters, Maggie, Tanetta, Annie, and Bessie, on ahead. He saw them settled into their cabin aboard the luxurious French liner *Ville du Havre*. Then he said good-bye, promising to join them soon.

The *Ville du Havre* never made it to London. In the early hours of November 22, 1873, it collided with an iron sailing vessel and water engulfed the ship in a matter of minutes. It was reported that screams, prayers, and oaths merged into the nightmare of unmeasured terror.

Passengers clung to whatever they could grab, tumbled through darkness, and were swept away by powerful currents of icy ocean. Loved ones fell from each other's grasp and disappeared into foaming blackness. Within two hours, the ship was gone beneath the waters. The 226 fatalities included Maggie, Tanetta, Annie, and Bessie. Mrs. Spafford was found clinging to a piece of the wreckage. When the forty-seven survivors landed in Cardiff, Wales, she cabled her husband with these words: "Saved alone!"

Horatio immediately booked passage to join his wife. While on his own voyage on a cold December night, the captain called him aside and said, "I believe we are now passing over the place where the *Ville du Havre* went down." Going to his cabin, Spafford could not sleep. He said to himself, "It is well; the will of God be done" (Morgan, *Then Sings My Soul*, p. 185).

Later, this man—torn by all his losses, yet trusting in His great Redeemer and lover of his soul—would write this most powerful and, for many of us, incomprehensible hymn, "It Is Well with My Soul."

When peace like a river, attendeth my way,
When sorrows like sea billows roll;
Whatever my lot, Thou has taught me to say,
"It is well, it is well, with my soul."

Though Satan should buffet, though trials should come,
Let this blest assurance control,
That Christ has regarded my helpless estate,
And has shed his own blood for my soul.

My sin—O the bliss of this glorious thought!
My sin, not in part, but the whole,
Is nailed to the cross, and I bear it no more;
Praise the Lord, praise the Lord, O my soul!

O Lord haste the day when the faith shall be sight,
The clouds be rolled back like a scroll,
The trump shall resound and the Lord shall descend,
"Even so"—it is well with my soul.

—*Trinity Hymnal*, p. 691

Who of us would write such a hymn after having lost, in such a brief span of time, all of our children and everything we were counting on to carry us into the future? We seem to be negatively impacted by our circumstances. In fact, situations and relationships are so powerful that they, at times, completely block out the greater goodness of a sovereign God who is using everything to cause our lives to be conformed to the image of Christ Jesus. Horatio Spafford seems to have understood this in his hymn. He did not just talk about the trials that come into our lives, but he immediately looked to Jesus, who, he said, "has regarded my helpless estate," and declared that Christ's death for him was the thing that changed the way he looked at everything.

Spafford may have lost his children and his earthly possessions, but his own sinfulness was his greatest concern, for *that* could destroy him for all eternity, not just bring sadness in this present life.

James 1:2–3 (*AB*) says, "Consider it wholly joyful, my brethren, whenever you are enveloped in or encounter trials of any sort or fall into various temptations. Be assured *and* understand that the trial *and* proving of your faith bring out endurance *and* steadfastness *and* patience. But let endurance *and* steadfastness *and* patience have full play *and* do a thorough work, so that you may be [people] perfectly and fully developed [with no defects], lacking in nothing." This is God's design for our lives. Trusting Him produces a life that does not lack any spiritual quality. This—coupled with the fact that our sin has been done away with, "not in part, but the whole," as Spafford declares—indeed causes us to be able to say, "It is well with my soul." Pretty amazing!

As we close this section on trust, we must look briefly at Psalm 37. In this Psalm, we are given a litany of things we should do in a world that seeks to consume us and cause us to despair. At the center of everything, we are encouraged to *trust*. The only way we can accomplish the other things set forth is by a firm, committed, consistent trust in the God of creation and redemption.

> Trust (lean on, rely on, and be confident) in the Lord and do good; so shall you dwell in the land and feed surely on His faithfulness, *and* truly you shall be fed. Delight yourself also, in the Lord, and He will give you the desires *and* secret petitions of your heart. Commit your way to the Lord [roll and repose each care of your load on Him]; trust (lean on, rely on, and be confident) also in Him and He will bring it to pass. And He will make your uprightness *and* right standing with God go forth as the light, and your justice *and* right as [the shining sun of]

the noonday. Be still *and* rest in the Lord; wait for Him *and* patiently lean yourself upon Him; fret not yourself. (Psalm 37:3–7 AB)

Trust! This is what we are to do. Every day that we live, we must practice this. Before we step out of our beds, we should ask the Lord God, by the power of the Holy Spirit, to enable us to *trust him* today. God is alive with power and wisdom, and He is with us in every event and relationship we face. Do not despair. Do not worry. Do not wonder. He will make Himself known, and He will deliver. Believe! Rest! Trust! Praise!

God of my hope,
God of my need,
God of my pain that no one else will ever see ...
God of my everything

(chorus of "God of My Everything" by Bebo Newman)

Chapter 5

Praying

As we read through the gospels in the New Testament and watch the disciples living in the physical presence of Jesus Christ, the Son of God, we would think that they would always be asking Him questions, seeking to understand the great mysteries of life. However—other than demonstrating their lack of faith, crying out for Him to save them, and seeking to assume elevated positions of power—one of their only personal requests of Him was, "Lord, teach us to pray" (Luke 11:1).

The disciples had seen Jesus turn water into wine, make the lame walk, give sight to the blind, quiet a raging storm, rejuvenate a leper's body, and raise the dead. In the midst of this, they wanted to know how to pray. They must have understood that Jesus' power source came from His deep and intimate relationship with the Father. All those times Jesus spent in prayer—only a small portion of which are recorded for us in Scripture—were what the disciples saw reviving and empowering the One they were following. Apparently, they saw prayer as a crucial act, and they wanted it to become part of their own lives.

In this final chapter, we are getting ready to tackle the subject of prayer. It is vital. If we are not men and women of prayer, we cannot walk, run, fight, or trust. In order to do all those things, we must be constantly engaged in prayer. We all know this. We all would agree and say amen. The difficulty is that most people, including believers, don't know anything about having a consistent, powerful, life-changing prayer life. Prayer is something we all know we should do, but few regularly engage in it.

Former chaplain of the US Senate, Richard Halverson, told the story of a time when the subject of prayer in schools was brought up before a senator who was giving an address to a church's annual men's dinner. The senator asked the men present how many of them believed in prayer in the public schools. Almost every man present raised his hand in the affirmative. Then the Senator asked, "How many of you pray daily with your own children in your home?" Out of several hundred men, only a few raised their hands (Michael P. Green, *Illustrations for Biblical Preaching* [Grand Rapids, Mich.: Baker Book House, 1990], 273).

Someone has said, "Prayer is the only omnipotence God grants to us" (*Illustrations*, 280). It is not my intention to try to teach you how to pray or to make you pray, but I do want us to consider the things we are to pray for and to understand the great power available to us. The only way you and I learn how to pray is to pray. If you want to learn to pray and you want to pray, then *pray*. Just *do* it! There is no secret formula to praying, only the actual doing of the deed. If you are not praying, please don't whine about not having the time or not knowing how. Fall on your knees or on your face, and cry out to God to help you and give you the grace to be broken and humbled before Him. Just talk to Him.

We are going to study the prayer that Jesus gave His disciples when they asked Him to teach them to pray, looking for the elements that should be present in our own prayers. We want to grasp what we should be praying for and how that will, in turn, direct our perspective of the lives we live. Let's not forget that we are commanded to "pray without ceasing" (1 Thessalonians 5:17). Our spiritual lives depend on it.

In the classic work on prayer by E. M. Bounds, he says, "We must pray so that our prayers take hold of God. The man who has done the most and the best praying is the most immortal, because prayers do not die. Perhaps the lips that uttered them are closed in death, or the heart that felt them may have ceased to beat, but the prayers live before God and God's heart is set on them. Prayers outlive the lives of those who uttered them—outlive a generation, outlive an age, outlive a world" (E. M. Bounds, *E. M. Bounds on Prayer* [New Kensington, Penn.: Whitaker House, 1997], 11). There is power in prayer, and it is the very thing that will cause us to walk, to run, to fight, and to trust.

A story is told of a couple who, years ago, said good-bye to their home church, as they were going to an African mission field known as "the white man's grave." The husband, in addressing the church, said, "My wife and I have a strange dread in going. We feel much as if we were going down into a pit. We are willing to take the risk and go if you, our home church, will promise to hold the ropes." All promised to do so.

Over the next year and a half, the wife and their only child died of a terrible fever. The husband, realizing that he too was dying of the same fever, returned home. Not having sent word of his return, he came to the Wednesday prayer meeting of his home church. He slipped in unnoticed and sat in the back. At the close of the meeting, he went forward. They looked at him and were dismayed, as they saw death written on his face.

He said, "I am your missionary. My wife and child are buried in Africa, and I have come home to die. This evening I listened anxiously as you prayed for some mention of your missionary to see if you were keeping your promise, but in vain! You prayed for everything connected with yourselves and your home circle, but you forgot your missionary. I see now why I am a failure as a missionary. It is because you have failed to hold the ropes" (*Illustrations for Biblical Preaching*, p. 280).

It may be that the missionary's conclusion was not right. He actually didn't fail as a missionary. However, his emphasis on the importance of prayer was correct. What great power we possess! How are we to wield it? Is it necessary for us to pray for missionary work around the world? As people who name the name of Christ, what should we be praying for?

God-Centered Matters

Jesus began teaching His disciples about prayer by turning their attention to the God they were to address. If we are going to walk, run, fight, and trust, it is very important to understand that all of our petitioning and supplication is to be done through the power and might of the living God. We are to acknowledge that our lives are lived in the presence of that one who is our Father and who rules from heaven: "Our Father who is in heaven" (Matthew 6:9).

Remember the day the followers of Jesus Christ were caught up in a discussion of who was the greatest in the kingdom of God? Jesus called a child to Himself and set the child before His disciples. This is the instruction Jesus gave to them: "Truly I say to you, unless you are converted and become like children, you will not enter the kingdom of heaven. Whoever then humbles himself as this child, he is the greatest in the kingdom of heaven" (Matthew 18:3–5).

In the early stages of life, children always have their attention focused on their parents. They are completely dependent upon others to provide for them, protect them, perform for them, and do all the necessary, daily functions that enable them to live. They run to their parents to seek everything they need to exist. Jesus immediately turned the disciples' attention to their heavenly parent, "our Father." He was making it clear that their first priority, even in prayer, was to consider their infinite, eternal, all-powerful, all-wise, and glorious Father.

It appears that in referring to a childlike attitude as essential to being part of the kingdom of God, Christ stresses one specific characteristic of children: humility. At first we might question this, knowing the independent spirit expressed by so many children today. However, I believe that Jesus was speaking about children in the earliest period of their lives, when they are fed by their parents and picked up and carried in their arms, when their parents are the only ones who can really meet their deepest needs of hunger, hurt, and helplessness, when children are dependent upon the adults they know as "mommy" and "daddy."

I believe this is exactly the attitude that Jesus was declaring that we need each day as we come into the presence of the God of the universe, who is also our Father. Jesus said that this is true for those who are "*converted* and become like children" (Matthew 18:3, emphasis mine). Just because we have been made in the image of God does not mean we can call God "our Father." There must be a transference, a conversion that takes us from one kingdom, the kingdom of darkness, to another kingdom, the kingdom of light, on the basis of our repentance and faith. Once this has happened, our continued relationship is that of a humble child who comes to his or her Father to seek Him, desiring His wisdom and power.

One of the greatest definitions of humility that I have ever come across is by Andrew Murray. I have used this definition over and over in my leadership development curriculum, my men's discipleship materials, and my teaching through books of the Bible, and any time the subject comes up. I am sure that it comes from Murray's book, *Humility: The Beauty of Holiness.* If you read this book, it will be a great blessing to you. Here is the definition *humility*:

"Humility is perfect quietness of heart. It is to expect nothing, to wonder at nothing done to me, to feel nothing done against me. It is to be at rest when nobody praises me, and when I am blamed or despised. It is to have a blessed home in the Lord, where I can go and shut the door, and kneel to my Father in secret, and am at peace as in a deep sea of calmness, when all around and above is trouble. The humble person is not one who thinks meanly [lowly] of himself, he simply does not think of himself at all" (Andrew Murray, *Humility: The Beauty of Holiness*).

Of course, the greatest example of this kind of humility—and especially as it pertains to coming into the presence of God, as a son before His Father—is Jesus Christ Himself. We are given a blow-by-blow description of what this looks like when one "does not think of himself at all." The apostle Paul said to the Philippians,

> Do nothing from selfishness or empty conceit, but with humility of mind, regard one another as more important than yourselves; do not merely look out for your own personal interests, but also for the interests of others. Have this attitude in yourselves which was also in Christ Jesus, Who, although He existed in the form of God, did not regard equality with God a thing to be grasped, but emptied Himself, taking the form of a bond-servant, and being made in the likeness of men. Being found in appearance as a man, He humbled Himself by becoming obedient to the point of death, even death on a cross. (Philippians 2:3–8)

This is the greatest Father-and-Son relationship ever revealed. Here is the Son, coming before the Father in humility, completely dependent and completely obedient. When we come before the

God who rules over all nations and all mankind, we have the glorious privilege of coming as sons and daughters before Him who is "our Father." "But as many as received Him, to them He gave the right to become *children* of God, even to those who believe in His name" (John 1:12, emphasis mine).

As children we come with the same attitude as the eternal Son, completely dependent and completely obedient, humility ruling our minds, emotions, and behavior. As we pray this way, it has a powerful effect upon daily walking, running, fighting, and trusting. We become different people, people who look more and more like Christ Himself. In case the obvious escapes us, this is a good thing.

The second line of the Lord's Prayer is also pregnant with a God-centered focus: "Hallowed be Your name" (Matthew 6:9b). The first line reminds us of a tender and intimate relationship with the one who is the sovereign Creator, Ruler, and Redeemer, but this line takes us into the very core of the character and nature of the one we are addressing. *Hallowed* literally means "to make holy" (W. E. Vine, *Vine's Expository Dictionary of Biblical Words* [Nashville: Thomas Nelson Publishers, 1978], 287).

Jesus told His disciples to "make holy" or "keep holy" the name of His Father. Of course, the whole concept of one's name, from the standpoint of Scripture, signifies a person's character and nature. As supplicants, we are to acknowledge the essence of who God is and keep in the forefront of our minds that we are addressing the one and only, true and living God. We are not talking to Santa Claus. We are not speaking to Buddha, Allah, or any other manmade god. We are talking to the Creator of the universe, the Sovereign God of redemption, the triune God of the Bible, the one who is eternal, infinite, omnipotent, omnipresent, the Most High God who rules in the kingdom of men.

In previous pages, I recorded Scripture verses and a quote referring to the glorious makeup of the God who has revealed Himself to us. The second paragraph of the *Westminster Confession of Faith*, chapter 2, "Of God, and of the Holy Trinity," says,

> God hath all life, glory, goodness, blessedness, in and of himself; and is alone in and unto himself all-sufficient, not standing in need of any creatures which he hath made, nor deriving any glory from them, but only manifesting his own glory in, by, unto, and upon them: he is the alone foundation of all being, of whom, through whom, and to whom are all things; and hath most sovereign dominion over them, to do by them, for them, or upon them, whatsoever himself pleaseth. In his sight all things are open and manifest; his knowledge is infinite, infallible, and independent upon the creature, so as nothing is to him contingent or uncertain. He is most holy in all his counsels, in all his works, and in all his commands. To him is due from angels and men, and every other creature, whatsoever worship, service, or obedience he is pleased to require of them.

Do you see what Jesus was doing here? He was showing us the intimate relationship we have with God as our Father and, at the same time, the utter respect, honor, and glory we are to give to Him. This relationship is pictured in the book of Revelation. We come and fall down before the one who is our Father, the one who must always be acknowledged as holy in our hearts and minds. "And the four living creatures, each one of them having six wings, are full of eyes around and within; and day and night they do not cease to say, "Holy, holy is the Lord God, the Almighty, who was and who is to come."

And when the living creatures give glory and honor and thanks to Him who sits on the throne, to Him who lives forever and ever, the twenty-four elders will "fall down before Him who sits on the throne, and will cast their crowns before the throne saying, 'Worthy are You, our Lord and our God, to receive glory and honor and power; for You created all things, and because You will they existed and were created'" (Revelation 4:8–11).

Prayer is to bring us into this God-centered relationship and God-centered perspective, which immediately give us a position of power, strength, hope, peace, comfort, rest, calmness, joy, and trust. The prophet Isaiah said it best when he spoke God's Word to His people: "Do not fear, for I am with you; do not anxiously look about you, for I am your God. I will strengthen you, surely I will help you, surely I will uphold you with my Righteous right hand" (Isaiah 41:10). The apostle Paul made this even more clear when he said: "Be anxious for nothing, but in everything by prayer and with supplication with thanksgiving, let your requests be made known to God. And the peace of God, which surpasses all comprehension, will guard your hearts and minds in Christ Jesus" (Philippians 4:6–7).

Jesus said that this is where we begin in our prayers. We are to focus on God's character and the wonderful relationship we have with the living God who is our Father. Everything else flows out of this realization, including the first words that come out of our mouths. Nothing comes forth from us until we have acknowledged the reality of the one who has adopted us, saved us, and revealed Himself to us. There can be no walking, running, fighting, or trusting until we have seen this and known this.

A man rose in a meeting in the early 1900s and gave the following testimony: "I got off at the Pennsylvania depot as a tramp, and for a year I begged on the streets for a living. One day I touched a man on the shoulder and said, 'Mister, please give me a dime.' As soon as I saw his face, I recognized my father. 'Father, don't you know me?' I asked. Throwing his arms around me, he cried, 'I have found you; all I have is yours.' Men, think of it, that I, a tramp stood begging my father for ten cents, when for eighteen years he had been looking for me to give me all he was worth!" (*Knights Master Book of New Illustrations*, 207).

This is what Jesus was saying to His disciples. You have a heavenly Father who is the all-sufficient God. Always speak to Him first, think of Him first, and be overwhelmed with His wonder and goodness. He desires to give you all that He is.

Kingdom Matters

As Jesus continued to instruct His disciples in how to pray, He moved into the area of the Father's kingdom (Matthew 6:10). In fact, in the last part of Matthew 6, in dealing with the daily concerns of life, we are told what really matters: "For this reason I say to you, do not be worried about your life, as to what you will eat or what you will drink; nor for your body, as to what you will put on. Is not life more than food, and the body more than clothing? Look at the birds of the air, that they do not sow, nor reap, nor gather into barns, and yet your heavenly Father feeds them. Are you not worth much more than they? And who of you by being worried can add a single hour to his life? ... Do not worry then, saying, 'What will we eat?' or 'What will we drink?' or 'What will we wear for clothing?' *But seek first His kingdom and His righteousness*, and all these things will be added to you" (Matthew 6:25–33, emphasis mine).

The first gospel in the New Testament opens with the one who was sent to be Jesus' forerunner. John preached, "Repent, for the kingdom of heaven is at hand" (Matthew 3:2). After John's proclamation, Jesus began His earthly ministry by declaring,

"Repent for the kingdom of heaven is at hand" (Matthew 4:17). The kingdom of God is, rightly, the focus of our lives. We are to have a kingdom mind-set, which affects our priorities. A kingdom is made up of many people. We begin to prioritize those other people becoming part of the kingdom and bowing before the King in worship, adoration, and obedience. The "I" or "me" of my life takes a backseat to the "you" and "they" and "we" of the kingdom.

It's a shame that we so often relegate the historic battle of David and Goliath to children's church or to a children's Sunday school lesson. We must understand that this was never God's intention. It is one of the great biblical accounts of what should matter most in our lives: putting the glory and honor of God's kingdom before the selfish, self-centered tendencies that so often plague our own existence.

This is the account of the epic struggle between David, who represented God's theocratic nation, Israel, and Goliath, who acted for the nation of the Philistines, a pagan, wicked, and godless nation. Get the picture? What was David, a young teenage boy, going to do when he went to the camp of the Israelites, located opposite the Philistines, and saw their champion, Goliath, come out and taunt the living God? What are *we* doing as we walk, run, fight, and trust in the midst of a world that hates us and our Christ and acts as the kingdom of darkness against the kingdom of light?

David wanted to know what was going on. He asked, "What will be done for the man who kills this Philistine and takes away the reproach from Israel? For who is this uncircumcised Philistine, that he should taunt the armies of the living God?" (1 Samuel 17:26). Who was this "uncircumcised Philistine"? He had no power or authority over the armies of the living God. He had no covenant relationship to the all-sufficient, all-powerful God. Israel was God's nation! This world was God's world! The honor of His kingdom was at stake.

We are to possess a kingdom mind-set like David's. "Your kingdom come. Your will be done on earth as it is in heaven" (Matthew 6:10). Of course, it is a spiritual kingdom we are presently praying for, but the reality of it is of no less important than the theocratic kingdom of Israel in the Old Testament.

After declaring that he had already killed a lion and a bear to protect his father's sheep (I Samuel 17:33–37) and that the Lord had delivered him, David was certain that the Lord would again preserve him, because this "uncircumcised Philistine" was taunting the armies of God. It was as if David was saying, "Don't you understand? God is concerned for His nation and that His honor and glory will stand and not be offended."

Do we pray with the same conviction? Are we certain that God's glory will be seen and affirmed, even if it doesn't fully take place until that day when "at the name of Jesus every knee will bow, of those who are in heaven and on earth and under the earth, and that every tongue will confess that Jesus Christ is Lord, to the glory of God the Father" (Philippians 2:10–11).

With his sling and his "five smooth stones," David walked down to meet Goliath on the field of battle. The giant was full of anger because they had sent a boy to fight him. He cursed David and told him that he was going to "give his [David's] flesh to the birds of the sky, and the beasts of the field."

David responded from the perspective of his covenant King, who was sovereign and ruled over all: "You come to me with a sword, a spear, and a javelin, but I come to you in the name of the LORD of hosts, the God of the armies of Israel, whom you have taunted. This day the LORD will deliver you up into my hands, and I will strike you down and remove your head from you. And I will give the dead bodies of the army of the Philistines this day to the birds of the sky and the wild beasts of the earth that all the earth may know that there is a God in Israel, and that all this assembly may know that the LORD does not deliver by sword or by spear; for the battle is the LORD'S and He will give you into our hands" (1 Samuel 17:41–47).

Where did we ever get the idea that this is just a great children's story about a young boy killing a giant? This is kingdom business. This is about standing for the truth and honor of the glory of God. This is about shouting to the world that we, God's people, the spiritual kingdom of God on this earth, have a God who is mighty and powerful and cannot be defeated. Kingdom business means declaring to a fallen, dark world that there is a God of light who ultimately wins and that all those who oppose Him will one day be delivered into His hands. He is the Lord of Hosts. He is the Most High God who rules in the kingdom of men. Nothing can stand in His way. Nothing can thwart His purposes. The world, with all of its giants, *will lose*. The kingdom of God conquers all!

I'm sure we all know the end of this historic account between David and Goliath. "Thus David prevailed over the Philistine with a sling and a stone, and he struck the Philistine and killed him ... Then David ran and stood over the Philistine and took his [Goliath's] sword and drew it out of its sheath and killed him, and cut off his head with it" (1 Samuel 17:50–51). Pretty decisive, wouldn't you say?

It was not only David who exemplified a man of God. Even a pagan king like Nebuchadnezzar came to understand and acknowledge that the God of Israel was the true King and that his own reign meant nothing. Daniel interpreted Nebuchadnezzar's dream, which told him that, because of his pride, he would be removed from being king for seven years, that he would "be driven away from mankind," and that his dwelling place would be "with the beasts of the field," where he would "be given grass to eat like cattle and be drenched with the dew of heaven" (Daniel 4:25). We are told that "all this happened to Nebuchadnezzar the king" (4:28).

Then we have this great testimony by Nebuchadnezzar, recorded for us from his own mouth: "But at the end of that period, I Nebuchadnezzar, raised my eyes toward heaven, and my reason returned to me, and I blessed the Most High and praised and honored Him who lives forever; for His dominion is an everlasting dominion, and His Kingdom endures from generation to generation. All the inhabitants of the earth are accounted as nothing, but He does according to His will in the host of heaven and among the inhabitants of earth, and no one can ward off His hand or say to Him, 'What have you done?'" (Daniel 4:34–35). Nebuchadnezzar's life was no longer about himself. Life was about the true King who had made Himself known to the king of Babylon.

Even as we think about the teachings of Jesus Christ, we realize that His emphasis was on instructing those who gathered around Him with "kingdom parables." When the disciples asked Jesus why He was teaching in parables, His answer was: "To you it has been granted to know the mysteries of the kingdom of heaven, but to them it has not been granted" (Matthew 13:11). Living is kingdom business, and we are to have a kingdom mind-set. What does this do in practice? When it comes to the individual believer's thoughts and actions, this mind-set means: God first, others second, and myself third!"

Jesus did exactly what the Father wanted Him to do. He went through towns and villages and taught in the synagogues, "proclaiming the gospel of the kingdom" (Matthew 9:35). Then this sobering picture is painted for us. "Seeing the people, He felt compassion for them, because they were distressed and dispirited like sheep without a shepherd. Then He said to His disciples,

'The harvest is plentiful, but workers are few. Therefore beseech the Lord of the harvest to send out workers into His harvest'" (Matthew 9:36–38).

What are we to be praying for? Where is our attention to be directed? It is the harvest! The building up of the kingdom of God is to be our concern. There are people separated from God, distressed and downcast. There are those who are in trouble and hurting. Christ's great compassion is to be shared by those who are His. All the stumbling blocks of our own lives pale in comparison to the great need around us and the potential gathering-in of the harvest.

Some of the last recorded words of Christ on this earth were what we call the "Great Commission" or the "Great Commandment." These were kingdom words. Backed by Jesus' authority in heaven and on earth, He commanded, "Go therefore and make disciples of all the nations, baptizing them in the name of the Father and the Son and the Holy Spirit, teaching them to observe all that I command you; and lo, I am with you always even to the end of the age" (Matthew 28:19–20).

This is the harvest! Making disciples is all about the kingdom. This is what we are praying for and what we are doing. We are not living for ourselves. Whatever our relationships—as husband, wife, son, daughter, grandson, granddaughter, coworker, friend, neighbor, or relative—we are praying for others, speaking to them and longing that they become disciples in the kingdom of God and products of a great harvest. Why?

The story is told of Harry Winston. Harry was one of the world's greatest jewel merchants. One of his salesmen was showing a beautiful diamond to a rich Dutch merchant. Listening carefully to the expert description of the diamond, the customer eventually turned away, saying, "It is a wonderful stone, but not exactly what I want." Before the merchant could leave, Winston himself stopped him and asked, "Do you mind If I show you the diamond once more?" The customer agreed.

Winston took the stone in his hand. As he spoke, he did not repeat anything the salesman had said. Instead, he simply spoke about the diamond as an object of great beauty. Suddenly the customer changed his mind and bought the gem. As it was being polished and prepared for his reception, he turned to Winston and said, "Why did I buy it willingly from you, though I had no difficulty saying no to your salesman?"

Winston replied, "That salesman is one of the best men in the business. He knows diamonds—but I love them" (*Illustrations for Biblical Preaching*, 125).

The reason we work in the "harvest" is because we love Jesus Christ. We love the King of the kingdom. Of course, we love Him because He has loved us so gloriously, wonderfully, and completely. Even in the midst of our helpless and ungodly state, Christ died for us (Romans 5:6). While we were sinners, the very enemies of God, Christ reconciled us and brought us into a relationship of peace and acceptance with the Most High God who rules in the kingdom of men (Romans 5:1, 8, 10). The kingdom of God becomes the most important thing in our lives.

We love the King. We love the kingdom. We pray that this kingdom will spiritually rule in hearts and lives, knowing that one day it will be actualized physically when Jesus Christ comes back again: "But when the Son of Man comes in His glory, and all the angels with Him, then He will sit on His glorious throne. All the nations will be gathered before Him; and He will separate them from one another, as the shepherd separates the sheep from the goats; and He will put the sheep on His right, and the goats on the left" (Matthew 25:31-33).

Kingdom matters matter! They are far more important than my wants and demands. What pertains to the kingdom is eternal.

What pertains to the things of this world is temporal. Kingdom-mindedness is a far greater help to me for living in this world than worldly-mindedness. In the book of Revelation, the apostle John was in the midst of his heavenly vision and was being shown what truly mattered. He saw the Lamb of God take the book, which no one but the Lamb could open, and "the four living creatures and the twenty-four elders" fell down "before the Lamb, each one holding a harp and golden bowls full of incense, which are the prayers of the saints" (Revelation 5:8). At this point, those who were mentioned sang a new song to the Lamb: "Worthy are You to take the book and to break the seals; for You were slain, and purchased for God with Your blood men from every tribe and tongue and people and nation. You have made them to be a kingdom of priests to our God; and they will reign upon the earth" (Revelation 5:9–10). Ultimately, what we possess—our bank accounts, our homes, our cars, and our toys—matter not. What matters is the kingdom of God and that we are part of that kingdom, seeking that others might also know, worship, and honor our King.

Personal Matters

The next thing we notice about the Lord's Prayer is that there are three matters we should prioritize in regard to ourselves. It is important to notice that these concerns are not self-centered or self-seeking. They are requested within the context of our relationship to our heavenly Father and His kingdom. We don't partake of our "daily bread" without realizing that the Lord God is the provider. He determines our ultimate purpose as He provides for us, and as we are eating, we are to keep the kingdom of God before our eyes.

Provision

Provision is the first thing we are told to keep before us. We pray, "Give us this day our daily bread" (Matthew 7:11). Our prayer seeks that the Lord God provide "bread" for us. Of course, a person can't live on bread alone, so this must refer to all that an individual would need on a daily basis to live. Physically, we need food, water, clothing, and shelter in order to live. These are the basic things necessary for the sustaining of life. "Bread" would not be defined as money, jobs, bank accounts, homes, cars, gadgets, or toys. We can and should pray about the physical necessities of life, realizing that God Himself daily provides us with these. When we bow our heads over a meal and thank the Lord for providing us with the food we are about to eat, this is not just a nice gesture or an optional practice on our part. We actually have the privilege and the obligation to acknowledge, with grateful hearts, what has been given to us.

Even though Jesus appears to have been talking principally about physical nourishment and sustenance, I think He was also referring to spiritual food. Our spiritual lives are just as dependent upon "food" as our physical lives are. In Matthew 4, Jesus was led into the wilderness and had been fasting for "forty days and forty nights" (v. 2). The tempter, the great usurper and Father of Lies, came to Jesus and said, "If You are the Son of God, command that these stones become bread" (v. 3).

Jesus answered, "It is written, 'Man shall not live on bread alone, but on every word that proceeds out of the mouth of God'" (v. 4). Of course, Jesus was referring to the Old Testament passage in Deuteronomy, where Moses reminded the people of Israel that they were wandering in the wilderness, not only because of their disobedience, but because God wanted to humble them and make them understand that the words of God are as necessary for life as physical bread (Deuteronomy 8:1–3).

So, in effect, we don't just pray for the bread that comes in loaves. We also ask God to give us His Word, which He speaks to us through the writings of His prophets and apostles. We need truth to live. When we drive down the highway and encounter a sign that says, "Dangerous Curve Ahead," we are immediately confronted with a choice. We can observe the warning and slow down, ignore the warning and maintain the same rate of speed, or we can defy the warning and speed up. Whatever we do, we will not change the truth of the sign. The curve remains dangerous, whether or not we acknowledge that fact (*Illustrations for Biblical Preaching*, 390). However, we need the truth to be put before us in order to make a decision about what we are going to do.

The Scriptures, the written Word of God, claim for themselves this same truth-proclaiming quality: "All Scripture is inspired by God and profitable for teaching, for reproof, for correction, for training in righteousness; so that the man of God may be adequate, equipped for every good work" (2 Timothy 3:16–17). God's Word gives us truth for life and teaches us what we need to know about Him and His character, about ourselves and our relationship with Him, and about this world and how we should see it and think about it. At the same time that the Word corrects us and shows us what we shouldn't do, it reproves us and shows us what we *should* do. Then it trains us in the right way to live. All of this is done to equip us for "every good work." It is a pretty satisfying meal. More than physical bread, it actually sustains us and prepares us for life.

David Prager, a well-known social critic, was debating Jonathan Glove, the atheistic Oxford philosopher. Prager posed this question: "If you, Professor Glover, were stranded at the midnight hour on a desolate Los Angeles street, and if, as you stepped out of your car with fear and trembling, you were suddenly to hear the weight of pounding footsteps behind you, and you saw ten burly young men, who had just stepped out of a dwelling, coming toward you, would it or would it not make a difference to you to know they were coming from a Bible study?" (Robert J. Morgan, *Nelson's Complete Book of Stories, Illustrations and Quotes* [Nashville: Thomas Nelson Publishers, 2000], 55).

The story has been told of a South Sea islander who proudly displayed his Bible to a G. I. during World War II. "We've outgrown that sort of thing," the soldier said. The native smiled back and said, "It's a good thing we haven't. If it weren't for this book, you'd have been a meal by now" (*Illustrations for Biblical Preaching*, 29).

Both of the illustrations above show us the power and effect of the Word of God. This is to be our food. Daily, we are to draw from its truth and apply it to our lives. We are to read it over, think it through, write it down, pray it, live it out, and pass it on. We eat it, digest it, and allow it to pass through our lives and make us like Christ.

Of course, we have been talking about the written Word, but there is also the *living* Word. Jesus was talking to a crowd in John 6. He was actually rebuking them for seeking signs from Him instead of pursuing His person. Christ offered to give them food "which endures to eternal life" (v. 27). Jesus told them to believe in Him, but they wanted a sign. They said that Moses had given their ancestors manna in the wilderness.

But our Lord corrected them and said, "Truly, truly, I say to you, it is not Moses who has given you bread out of heaven, but it is my Father who gives you the true bread out of heaven. For the bread of God is that which comes down out of heaven, and gives life to the world" (John 6:32–33). Now, this was bread that they wanted! Jesus told them in jaw-dropping fashion, "I am the bread of life, he who comes to Me will not hunger, and he who believes in me will never thirst" (v. 35). We must taste and eat of Jesus if we are going to have life.

One of the greatest scenes from C. S. Lewis' *Chronicles of Narnia* is recorded in *The Silver Chair*. Remember that Aslan, the great lion, represented Jesus Christ. The encounter with Jill, a Son of Adam, goes like this:

> "Are you thirsty?" said the Lion.
>
> "I'm dying of thirst," said Jill.
>
> "Then drink," said the Lion.
>
> "May I—could I—would you mind going away while I do?" said Jill.
>
> The Lion answered this only by a look and a very low grow. And as Jill gazed at its motionless bulk, she realized that she might as well have asked the whole mountain to move aside for her convenience. The delicious rippling noise of the stream was driving her nearly frantic.
>
> "Will you promise not to do anything to me, if I do come?" said Jill."
>
> "I make no promises," said the Lion.
>
> Jill was so thirsty now that, without noticing it, she had come a step nearer.
>
> "Do you eat girls?" she said.
>
> "I have swallowed up girls and boys, women and men, kings and emperors, cities and realms," said the Lion. It did not say this as if it were boasting, nor as if it were sorry, nor as if it were angry. It just said it.
>
> "I daren't come and drink," said Jill.
>
> "Then you will die of thirst," said the Lion.
>
> "Oh dear!" said Jill, coming another step nearer. "I suppose I must go and look for another steam then."
>
> "There is no other stream," said the Lion.

—Wayne Martindale and Jerry Root, ed.,
The Quotable Lewis (Wheaton, Ill.:
Tyndale House Publishers, Inc.), 51

"There is no other stream!" Only Christ can give us life and quench our thirst. If we will not believe in Him, we will die. He is the only one who can cause us to live. He is our daily bread.

We all go through difficult and trying times. Over the past six years, my world has been turned upside down. So many times I have believed that I could not rise up and go forth. All of the trials and grief have centered around my family, whom I love more than I could ever express in words. Finally, I came to the place of realization that no one, not even family members, can give me life-giving water or bread that can sustain me. Only one person can do this, the one who actually died for me, covered my sin in His sacrificial blood, and clothed me in His glorious righteousness.

When this great truth dawned upon my cold, dead heart so that it became fresh and new, I penned the following words and taped the note in my Bible: "Everything that has happened in my life up to this point is a means for God's grace to strip me of my pride and to clothe me with humility, so that the Lamb of God might be formed in me—his meekness and his death—so that I become nothing and Christ becomes my all in all."

The Lamb of God is to be our portion. He is to be our daily bread. Christ is to become our all in all. The following is also taped to the flyleaf of my Bible. I do not remember where I got it. It is anonymous in its authorship, but I can't tell you how many times I have gone to it to remind myself of its penetrating truth.

Christ All in All

Christ for sickness, Christ for health,
Christ for poverty, Christ for wealth,
Christ for joy, Christ for sorrow,
Christ today, and Christ tomorrow,
Christ my life, Christ my light,

Christ for morning, noon, and night,
Christ when all around gives way,
Christ my everlasting stay,
Christ my rest and Christ my food,
Christ above my highest good,
Christ my well beloved, my friend,
Christ my pleasure, without end,
Christ my Savior, Christ my Lord,
Christ my portion, Christ my God
Christ my good shepherd, I His sheep,
Christ Himself my soul doth keep.
Christ my leader, Christ my peace,
Christ hath given my soul release,
Christ my righteousness divine,
Christ for me, for He is mine!
Christ my wisdom, Christ my meat,
Christ restores my wandering feet,
Christ my advocate and priest,
Christ who ne'er forgets the feast.
Christ my teacher, Christ my guide,
Christ my rock, in Christ I hide,
Christ the everlasting bread,
Christ His precious blood has shed,
Christ has brought me nigh to God,
Christ the everlasting Word,
Christ my master, Christ my head,
Christ who for my sins hath bled.
Christ my glory, Christ my crown,
Christ the plant of great renown,
Christ my comforter on high,
Christ my hope is ever nigh,
Christ is coming in the air,
Christ—Come quickly is my prayer!

What needs to be said after this? "Give us this day our daily bread."

Forgiveness

The next concern Jesus tells His disciples to pray about is their need for forgiveness and their practice of forgiving others. I have written a whole book on the subject of forgiveness, so I am not going to address its full implications and obligations again. What I do want to point out is that, even though this is under the general heading of "Personal Matters," we are still dealing with "Kingdom Matters" that focus on others and not ourselves. Forgiveness is not about *me*. It is about *others*. Jesus said, "And forgive *us our* debts, as *we* also have forgiven *our* debtors" (Matthew 7:12, emphasis mine). In the body of Christ, in the kingdom of God, forgiveness is to characterize all that we do and say.

We must continually and constantly receive the forgiveness of Christ. The word used in the Greek for *debts* and *debtors* is a legal term. As we figuratively stand before the bar of God, we legally owe Him, because of His holiness, payment for our sins. Punishment is due for our violation of the law of God. It is a debt that we owe, but the debt has been paid through the sacrifice and shed blood of Christ (*Vine's Expository Dictionary of Biblical Words*, 150). We seek Christ's forgiveness and, on the basis of our having been forgiven, we in like manner forgive those who have done wrong against us. Notice that "us," "our," and "we," are mentioned here. The whole body of Christ, representing the kingdom of God to the world, is to seek needed forgiveness and to promise to give that same forgiveness. The testimony the world sees must be that vivid and glorious reality of received and given forgiveness.

C. S. Lewis made this insightful observation: "To forgive the incessant provocations of daily life to keep forgiving the bossy mother-in-law, the bullying husband, the nagging wife, the selfish daughter, the deceitful son—how can we do it? Only, I think, by remembering where we stand, by meaning our words when we say in our prayers each night, 'Forgive us our trespasses as we forgive those that trespass against us.' We are offered forgiveness on no other terms. To refuse it is to refuse God's mercy for ourselves. There is no hint of exceptions and God means what He says" (*The Quotable Lewis*, 221).

The point is that if we refuse to forgive someone else, it means that we know nothing of Christ's forgiveness in our own lives. We have not accepted and received His forgiveness. He is not our Lord and Savior. There is no relationship between us and Christ. Christ's whole purpose in dying a criminal's death upon the cross was to exact the payment necessary to purchase pardon for sin-filled, iniquity-laden, vile enemies of God. We declare that we refuse this forgiveness when we do not forgive others. Forgiveness is not in our possession if we do not forgive, no matter what we profess. Lewis said, "We must forgive all our enemies or be damned" (*The Quotable Lewis*, 219).

Remember that Jesus was answering the request of His disciples when he taught them to pray. It is very instructive to see that Jesus put in this pattern of prayer this petition concerning forgiveness. We are caught up in the world we live in, so overwhelmed with external things, such as how we look and how we are performing, not just as employers and employees but as husbands and fathers, wives and mothers, sons and daughters. We need to be brought back to what is really important: what is going on inside of us. Forgiveness is an internal state of the mind and heart. It is a mater of the will, where we choose to set aside a wrong suffered. It is the actual practice of possessing the attitude of Christ (Philippians 2:5).

Humility is the birthplace of forgiveness. We are to do what we do from a humble mind-set regarding "one another as more important that ourselves" (Philippians 2:3). Our actions flow from the mind, from what we think. Right thinking leads to right behavior. We know that we deserve nothing but condemnation, and yet, according to God's free grace, we have been forgiven through the sacrifice of Christ. Therefore, our forgiveness should flow to others as we draw upon the power of God's indwelling Spirit, which represents the resurrected life of Christ in us.

In World War II, Corrie Ten Boom and her sister Betsie were arrested for concealing Jews and were sent to a German concentration camp. Betsie eventually died a slow and terrible death as a result of the cruel treatment she received. Then in 1947, Corrie spoke about God's forgiveness to a church in Munich. After her message, while greeting people, a man came forward, stretched out his hand, and said, "Ja, Fraulein, it is wonderful that Jesus forgives us all our sins, just as you say." She remembered his face as being one of the prison guards who had treated her sister so ruthlessly. He told her that he had become a Christian, and, with his hand still extended, he asked her to forgive him.

A great battle began to wage inside of her. Her hand was frozen. Then Matthew 6:15, the very last verse of the passage containing the Lord's Prayer, came flooding into her mind: "But if you do not forgive others, then your Father will not forgive your transgressions." She silently prayed, *Jesus, help me!* and thrust her hand into the hand of her former tormentor. She forgave as she had been forgiven (Robert J. Morgan, *Nelson's Complete Book of Stories, Illustrations, Quotes,* 315–316).

This is kingdom living! This is what it means to live as a Christian man or a Christian woman. So often, it is far less dramatic than the above illustration. Someone says something to us or about us. Something hurts our feelings, and we get angry, and a crack opens in our relationship with that person. Hurt feelings, wounded emotions, and relationships are torn apart. As the suffering and dying of Christ Jesus has forgiven us our rebellion and disobedience, nothing can stand in the way of our forgiving others. We must forgive, or we will not be forgiven. We say we belong to the kingdom of God. Then we are to live like it! Kingdom people are forgiven people who practice that same forgiveness toward others. We represent the King. The King is characterized by His all-glorious forgiveness. His character is to be the character of His subjects. No forgiveness, no King. No King, no hope!

Temptation and Evil

We are still praying a "kingdom prayer," and our focus is still on the kingdom of God. We are kingdom people, and our reason for being on planet Earth is to "make disciples" and see others become a part of Christ's kingdom (Matthew 28:19). However, we are at the part of the prayer that concerns our daily living as representatives of Christ's reign and the need to guard our hearts. Again, there is an individual aspect to this, but at the same time, we are still using plural pronouns: "Do not lead us into temptation" (Matthew 6:13a). If this "kingdom" is going to remain faithful to the King, then our concern at this point is not just for ourselves but for all who make up this realm.

In the Lord's Prayer it seems that Jesus is telling us that our heavenly Father is the author or source of temptations. Of course, we always attempt to understand a difficult verse in Scripture by allowing other portions of Scripture to interpret for us what something means. It is very clear in the epistle of James that God does not tempt anyone. "Let no one say when he is tempted, 'I am being tempted by God'; for God cannot be tempted by evil, and He Himself does not tempt any one" (James 1:13). Actually, we are tempted when each of us is "carried away and enticed by his own lust" (1:14). We also know that Satan is our tempter (1 Corinthians 7:5), just as he sought to tempt Christ in the wilderness (Mark 1:3).

So, what does Jesus mean when He tells us to ask the Father not to lead us into temptation? It would appear that Jesus was saying that we are to plead with the Father not to allow the temptation or testing, which will surely come, to cause us to fall. We ask that He not let us actually succumb or be overtaken or be led into the temptation. We ask that He give us victory over the temptation, aid us in our fight against it, and help all of those who are kingdom men and women to rise above the temptation.

Jesus Himself was tempted in the wilderness, but He did not yield. Someone has said, "In the three temptations Jesus made His basic decision. He fixed the path and spirit and method of His ministry. He refused to act out of selfish concern. He would not try to force sensational support from God. He would not surrender to Satan for apparent advantage that could only defeat His God-given purpose. He would take up His humble ministry, which would lead to the cross rather than to personal comfort, spectacular power, and worldly success" (E. Paul Hovey, ed., *The Treasury of Inspirational Anecdotes, Quotations, and Illustrations* [Grand Rapids, Mich.: Fleming H. Revell, 1994], 276).

It is important that we know the following: "Temptation is a part of life. No one is immune—at any age. For temptation is present wherever there is a choice to be made, not only between good and evil, but also between a higher and lower good. For some, it may be a temptation to sensual gratification; for others a temptation to misuse their gifts, to seek personal success at the cost of the general welfare, to seek a worthy aim by unworthy means, to lower their ideas to win favor with the electorate, or with their companions and associates" (*The Treasury of Inspirational Anecdotes*, 275).

So, how do we respond as Jesus did? How do we face temptation without coming under its seductive power? We need supernatural power. *God, help me!* becomes our cry. Jesus instructed us to petition the Father to protect us from temptation. An old Puritan said, "Temptation provokes me to look upward to God" (*The Treasury of Inspirational Anecdotes*, 276).

Temptation is the solicitation of the will. It is subtle, dangerous, and destructive. As 1 Peter says, "Be of sober spirit, be on the alert. Your adversary, the devil, prowls around like a roaring lion, seeking someone to devour." The world and our own sinful flesh are also seeking to suck the faith out of every individual and to lead each one into disobedience and all kinds of immoral and idolatrous behavior. In *Mere Christianity*, C. S. Lewis said: "A silly idea is current that good people do not know what temptation means. This is an obvious lie. Only those who try to resist temptation know how strong it is … We never find out the strength of the evil impulse inside of us until we try to fight it; and Christ, because He was the only man who never yielded to temptation, is also the only man who knows to the full what temptation means—the only complete realist" (pp. 124–125). Every day of our lives, we should seek to cry out to the living God for His power to fight against and flee from sin. This is why it is a pattern for our daily prayer.

It is not just ourselves that we are concerned about but all those who say they are followers of the King. If the members of the kingdom are allowing themselves to openly yield to temptation, it will reflect on the kingdom and, in turn and far more seriously, on the King. This is why, over the centuries, men and women have been willing to die for the glory and honor of the King, as opposed to giving in to the temptation to deny Christ and His cross. This great old hymn of the church is sung as a battle cry to keep ourselves strong and pure:

> Soldiers of Christ, arise,
> and put your armor on,
> Strong in the strength which God supplies,
> through His eternal Son.
> Strong in the Lord of Hosts,
> and in His mighty pow'r,
> Who in the strength of Jesus trusts
> is more than conqueror.
>
> Stand then in His great might,
> with all His strength endued;
> But take, to arm you for the fight,
> the panoply [complete armor] of God.
> Leave no unguarded place,
> no weakness of the soul;
> Take every virtue, every grace
> and fortify the whole.
>
> To keep your armor bright,
> attend with constant care;
> Still walking in your Captain's sight,
> and watching unto prayer.
> From strength to strength go on;
> wrestle and fight and pray;
> Tread all the pow'rs of darkness down,
> and win the well-fought day.
>
> —*Trinity Hymnal*, Atlanta: Great Commission
> Publications, 1990, 575

Jesus wanted His disciples to understand that the war with temptation was going to take the power of God to address. As James pointed out in his letter, temptation leads to sin, the breaking of God's commandments, either in our doing what He forbids or not doing what God instructs us to do (James 2:15). Sin, in turn, "brings forth death" (2:15). From a biblical perspective, this death describes physical, emotional, and eternal separation from the life and presence of God.

John Owen, in his treatise on "The Mortification of Sin" says, "Where sin ... gets considerable victory, it breaks the bones of the soul ... and makes a man weak, sick, and ready to die ... so that he cannot look up ... And when poor creatures will take blow after blow, wound after wound, foil after foil, and never rouse themselves to a vigorous opposition, can they expect anything but to be hardened through the deceitfulness of sin, and that their souls should bleed to death" (John Owen, *The Mortification of Sin* [Scotland: Christian Focus Publications, Genesis House, 2003], 33).

How important it is that we cry out to our Sovereign Father, "And do not lead us into temptation." Temptation is not something that kingdom people play around with. We do not seek it out, and it is that which we want to avoid. In fact, we will do everything to keep from it. This great hymn of the church should be our proposed bedrock, our conviction:

> Take my life, and let it be
> Consecrated, Lord, to Thee.
> Take my moments and my days,
> Let them flow in ceaseless praise.
> Let them flow in ceaseless praise.

Tale my hands, and let them move
At the impulse of Thy love.
Take my feet, and let them be
Swift and beautiful for Thee.
Swift and beautiful for Thee.

Take my voice, and let me sing,
Always, only, for my King.
Take my lips, and let them be
Filled with messages from Thee,
Filled with messages from Thee.
Take my silver and my gold;
Not a mite would I withhold.
Take my intellect, and use
Ev'ry pow'r Thou shalt choose,
Ev'ry pow'r Thou shalt choose.

Take my will and make it Thine;
It shall be no longer mine.
Take my heart, it is Thine own;
It shall be Thy royal throne,
It shall be thy royal throne.

Take my love; my Lord, I pour
At Thy feet its treasure store.
Take myself and I will be
Ever only, all for Thee,
Ever only, all for Thee.

—*Trinity Hymnal*, 585

Every aspect of our lives must be guarded, protected, and committed to the one who alone has the power to keep us from temptation.

However, it is not just temptation that we are to be concerned about. The last petition of the Lord's Prayer is that the Father would "deliver us from evil [literally "the evil one"] (Matthew 6:13b). The Evil One is real, and his whole purpose is to destroy our souls. He appeared in the first few chapters of the Bible, and the whole human race has been affected by his attack on Adam and Eve. He was referred to by Jesus in John 8:44 as "the Father of Lies." Eve was deceived by lies, not only in regard to what God had said but also in calling God a liar who didn't mean what He said. Knowing the hearts of men and women, even kingdom men and women, Jesus told His disciples that they should seek to be delivered from the one who delighted in confusing and deceiving and killing their trust and faith.

I think it would be helpful to quote a passage in John, where Jesus spoke specifically about the Devil. It is obvious that the Lord of glory, the Son of God, considers the Devil to be a real person. Jesus said, "If you are Abraham's children, do the deeds of Abraham. But as it is, you are seeking to kill Me, a man who has told you the truth, which I heard from God; this Abraham did not do. You are doing the deeds of your father … If God were your Father, you would love Me, for I proceed forth and have come from God, for I have not even come on my own initiative, but He sent Me. Why do you not understand what I am saying? It is because you cannot hear My word. You are of your father the devil, and you want to do the desires of your father. He was a murderer from the beginning, and does not stand in the truth because there is no truth in him. Whenever he speaks a lie [literally "*the* lie," which implies that he is always lying], he speaks from his own nature, for he is a liar and the father of lies" (John 8:39b–44).

We do not want anyone to keep us from loving Jesus by influencing us with lies. Even when Christ told His disciples that He was going to be killed and then raised the third day, Peter, because he appears to be listening to the "adversary," was rebuked with these words: "Get behind Me, Satan! You are a stumbling block to Me, for you are not setting your mind on God's interests, but man's" (Matthew 16:23).

We cannot set our minds and hearts on kingdom issues if Satan is motivating our thoughts and decisions. It is necessary—and Jesus knows this—for us to ask the all-powerful God to "deliver" us from daily evil and the Evil One who seeks to impose that evil upon us. We seem to be so naïve as we go through our daily routines. We have no active awareness in our lives that someone is seeking to conquer our thoughts with evil intentions. Wake up! Don't go to sleep! There is indeed one who "prowls around like a lion, seeking someone to devour" (1 Peter 5:8).

Of course, we have a perfect example of temptation and evil and its destructive power in the life of a man who wanted to be a faithful follower of His God: King David. David was referred to as "a man after His [God's] own heart" (1 Samuel 13:14). Yet in 2 Samuel 11, David did not go out to battle "at the time when kings go out to battle" but stayed in Jerusalem. At night he walked on the rooftop of his house and saw a woman bathing. At that very moment, David should have turned his eyes away and gone back to bed.

The epistle of James makes it very clear what actually happened. "But each one is tempted, when he is carried away and enticed by his own lust" (James 1:14). David should have cried out, "Oh, Lord God, lead me not into temptation. Lord, protect me! Let me walk away from the desire and passion of my own lust and go back to bed." Instead, the Bible says that "the woman was very beautiful in appearance. So David sent and inquired about the woman ... David sent messengers and took her" (1 Samuel 11:2–4).

Do you think, even though it is not specifically recorded, that the great enemy, the Father of Lies, was whispering in David's ear, "You're the king. You can do whatever you want.

This is your right!" Of course, David didn't just commit adultery with Bathsheba. He eventually had her husband killed and took her for himself. There was repentance in David's life over his shameful actions, but there were also great consequences for his sin. David's name appears in the list of the faithful in Hebrews 11:32, because God forgave him.

We are to sincerely pray these petitions in order to guard our hearts. We are kingdom men and women. We represent the King. We love the King. He is our Creator, Lord, and Savior. He has redeemed us. We have been transferred from the kingdom of darkness into the kingdom of light. Instead of condemnation, we have received new life in Christ. We do not want to break the heart of our King. We want to rejoice in Him and ever live our lives to honor, adore, and praise His name. Our lives must bless Him! We must ever live to declare His holiness and our utter dependence upon Him. Meditate on this great hymn by Isaac Watts.

> Jesus my great High Priest,
> Offered His blood and died;
> My guilty conscience seeks no sacrifice beside.
> His pow'rful blood did nonce atone,
> And now it pleads before the throne.
>
> To this dear Sure-ty's [Christ's] hand
> Will I commit my cause;
> He answers and fulfills His Father's broken laws.
> Behold my soul at freedom set;
> My Surety paid the dreadful debt.
>
> My Advocate appears
> For my defense on high;
> The Father bows His ears and lays His thunder by.
> Not all that hell or sin can say
> Shall turn His heart, His love away.

Should all the hosts of death
And pow'rs of hell unknown
Put their most dreadful forms of rage and mischief on,
I shall be safe, for Christ's displays
His conquering pow'r and guardian grace.

—"Jesus My Great High Priest,"
Trinity Hymnal, 306

The truth contained in this hymn causes us to be advocates of these last two petitions in the Lord's Prayer. The last phrase in the last stanza of "When I Survey the Wondrous Cross" sums it up: "Love so amazing, so divine, demands my soul, my life, my all (*Trinity Hymnal*, 252).

We do not want to break the law of God. We do not want to yield to the temptation of the Evil One. Our desire is to remain strong, ever a soldier of the cross, a conqueror of sin, a man or woman of God, and faithful member of the kingdom of God. Every day, all day long, we live to put on the armor of God and go forth to fight the battle for the supremacy of Christ in all things, especially in our thoughts, motives, and behavior. Sin and the Evil One are not our friends. They are our mortal enemies. We ever plead with our Father to keep them from our hearts.

Conclusion

Everything we have been discussing in this book has been related to preparation and readiness. We are such creatures of habit. Our days are spent in just trying to get by. There are certain things that lie before us, whether in our jobs or in the daily routine of getting our children to school, running errands, getting the children home from school, preparing meals, and handling all the other normal events of the day. We do these things without even considering that our lives are not just about our outward duties.

But we are spiritual beings made up of thoughts, emotions, and choices. We have enemies that seek to destroy our peace, hope, calm, understanding, trust, rational ability to see things as they really are, and everything that enables us to live gracious, forgiving, encouraging, loving lives. We must be ready! Walking, running, fighting, trusting, and praying are all part of the process in our preparation and equipping to live each day as more than conquerors.

Many of us seem to be so sophisticated and so enamored of the style of music in the twenty-first century. When we speak of the hymns of the church written in the 1700s and 1800s, we cringe and immediately discount them. That's too bad! Some of the greatest words and music adapted to congregational singing were written during this time. Many of these hymns not only contain great biblical theology but were also written in the midst of unique, God-directed circumstances. One such hymn is "Stand Up, Stand Up for Jesus."

Dudley Tyng was the assistant minister to his father at Philadelphia's Church of the Epiphany in 1854. At the age of twenty-nine, Dudley succeeded his father as pastor of this large Episcopal church. Everything went smoothly until Dudley began to preach vehemently against slavery. In 1856 he resigned.

Those who agreed with Dudley's position organized the Church of the Covenant in another part of the city, and his reputation grew. He began noontime Bible studies at the YMCA, and his ministry spread throughout the city of Philadelphia. Dudley had a great burden to lead husbands and fathers to Christ, and he helped organize a great rally to reach men.

On Tuesday, March 30, 1858, five thousand men gathered. Dudley looked out over the vast sea of men and, overwhelmed, he said to the crowd, "I would rather my right arm were amputated at the trunk than that I should fail in my duty to you in delivering God's message."

Over a thousand men came into the kingdom of God that day.

Two weeks later, Dudley was visiting in the countryside, watching a corn-thrasher at work in a barn. His hand moved too close to the blade and his sleeve got caught. His arm was ripped from the socket, the main artery severed. Four days later, his right arm was amputated close to his shoulder. As Dudley lay dying, he told his aged father, "Stand up for Jesus, Father, and tell my brethren of the ministry to stand up for Jesus."

Reverend George Duffield of Philadelphia's Temple Presbyterian Church was deeply stirred by Dudley's funeral, and the following Sunday he preached from Ephesians 6:14 about standing firm in Christ. He read a poem he had written, brought about by Dudley's final words.

The editor of a hymnal heard the poem, found appropriate music, and published it (Robert J. Morgan, *Then Sings My Soul*, 135). Here is the result of Dudley's dying words.

Stand up, stand up for Jesus, ye soldiers of the cross;
Lift high His royal banner, it must not suffer loss:
From victory unto victory His army He shall lead,
Till ev'ry foe is vanquished, and Christ is Lord indeed.

Stand up, stand up for Jesus, the trumpet call obey;
Forth to the might conflict in this His glorious day:
Ye that are men now serve Him against unnumbered foes;
Let courage rise with danger, and strength to
strength oppose.

Stand up, stand up for Jesus, stand in His strength alone;
The arm of flesh will fail you, ye dare not trust your own:
Put on the gospel armor, each piece put on with pray'r;
Where duty calls, or danger, be never wanting there.

Stand up, stand up for Jesus, the strife will not be long;
This day the noise of battle, the next the victor's song:
To him that over cometh a crown of life shall be;
He with the King of glory shall reign eternally.

—*Trinity Hymnal*, 571

How do we do this? How do we stand up, stand up for Jesus? It is accomplished by walking with God, running the race, fighting the good fight, trusting in the Lord, and praying all the time. None of this is just pie-in-the-sky by-and-by. This is not a self-help book. This is a book about battle tactics. There must be a constant drawing upon the inward power of the Holy Spirit working in our lives. We do not just try harder. We are not just trying to be better people. We are new creatures in Christ. A transformation, metamorphosis, has taken place. We live in a new kingdom, and we are new people.

I want to remind you of God's graphic picture of those who are His. It is so important that we see and know ourselves as God sees us and knows us, not as the godless world understands us—and not even as so many Christians today view themselves from a secular perspective rather than a biblical one. Because God's people were not living as God's people, He came and reminded them: "Your origin and your birth are from the land of Canaan; your father was an Amorite and your mother a Hittite" (Ezekiel 16:3). The only thing you need to know about your heritage is that you were born in sin. You derived your nature from those who are fallen, and you are fallen. Your nature is one of ungodliness and unrighteousness.

God went on to tell the people, "As for your birth, on the day you were born your navel cord was not cut, nor were you washed with water for cleansing; you were not rubbed with salt or even wrapped in cloths. No eye looked with pity on you to do any of these things for you, to have compassion on you. Rather you were thrown out into the open field, for you were abhorred on the day you were born" (Ezekiel 16:4–5). You were helpless and no one cared for you or loved you. You were abandoned and thrown out into the field to wallow in your own blood. This is also a spiritual picture of us now. We are lost, alone, and without hope. We will die in this state.

The description continues:

> "When *I* [the living God] passed by you and saw you squirming in your own blood, *I* said to you *while you were* in your blood, 'Live!' Yes. *I* said to you *while you were* in your blood, 'Live!' … Then *I* passed by you and saw you, and behold you were at the time for love; so *I* spread My skirt over you and covered your nakedness. *I* also swore to you and entered into a covenant with you so that you became Mine," declares the Lord God. "Then *I* bathed you with water, washed off your blood from you and anointed you with oil. *I* also clothed you with embroidered cloth and put sandals of porpoise skin on your feet; and *I* wrapped you with fine linen

and covered you with silk. *I* also put a ring in your nostril, earrings in your ears and a beautiful crown on your head." (Ezekiel 16:6, 8–12, emphasis mine)

This is one of the most glorious pictures of the grace of God in all of Scripture. Why would we not want every person to hear this? Why would we not want to tell everyone we speak with or counsel about this stupendous truth? God has done everything for us. He is the greatest king in the entire world. His love for us is beyond question, especially when you couple the description in Ezekiel with the cross of Christ. Nothing should stand in the way or cloud our judgment as we seek to return such love.

Yet I know my own heart. I know the struggle I have with pride, self-centeredness, spiritual adultery, and even idolatry itself. So I must draw upon a power outside of myself, a power placed within me by my King, who knows my weakness. He has given me His Spirit, the Holy Spirit, who gives me the ability to walk, the endurance to run, the courage to fight, the wisdom to trust, and the humility to pray. In Ezekiel 36, God said, "Moreover, *I* will give you a new heart and put a new spirit within you; and *I* will remove the heart of stone from your flesh and give you a heart of flesh. *I* will put My Spirit within you and cause you to walk in My statutes, and you will be careful to observe My ordinances … so you will be My people, and *I* will be your God" (Ezekiel 36:26–28, emphasis mine).

We have the strength of God Himself living within us to do the very things we need to do on a daily basis to be kingdom people. We do not do these things on our own. We are not trying to be better people. We seek to represent our King and lift up His name so that He can draw all people to Himself. Jesus Christ is always and forever our focus. It is His glory that we seek. The glory and honor of the King is our purpose. King Jesus is whom we live for and serve. This is why we walk, we run, we fight, we trust, and we pray. All of this takes place only because He gives us the grace and power to do so.

Reverend E. P. Scott, a missionary to India, told the story of his trying to reach a savage tribe in the Indian subcontinent. He went into this dangerous territory, ignoring the pleading of his friends. Several days into his journey, he met a large party of warriors who surrounded him, their spears pointed at his heart. Expecting to die at any moment, Scott took out his violin, breathed a prayer in his heart, and closed his eyes. As he played, he began to sing "All Hail the Power of Jesus' Name!" When he reached the words "let every kindred, every tribe," he opened his eyes. There stood the warriors, some in tears, every spear lowered. Scott spent the next two years evangelizing the tribe (Robert J. Morgan, *Then Sings My Soul*, 77).

Read the words of this great hymn:

> All hail the power of Jesus' name!
> Let angels prostrate fall;
> Bring forth the royal diadem,
> And crown Him Lord of all.
>
> Crown Him, ye martyrs of your God,
> Who from His altar call;
> Extol the Stem of Jesse's rod,
> And crown Him Lord of all.
>
> Ye seed of Israel's chosen race,
> Ye ransomed of the fall,
> Hail Him who saves you by His grace,
> And crown Him Lord of all.
>
> Sinners whose love can ne'er forget
> The wormwood and the gall,
> Go, spread your trophies at His feet,
> And crown Him Lord of all.

Let ev'ry kindred, ev'ry tribe,
On this terrestrial ball,
To Him all majesty ascribe,
And crown Him Lord of all.

O that with yonder sacred throng,
We at His feet may fall;
We'll join the everlasting song,
And crown Him Lord of all.

—*Trinity Hymnal*, 296
(the last line is repeated twice in each stanza)

This is our song. In the power of the Holy Spirit, we *walk* to hail the power of Jesus' name. We *run* to hail the power of Jesus' name. We *fight* to hail the power of Jesus' name; we *trust* to hail the power of Jesus' name. And we *pray* to hail the power of Jesus' name. We take all of our self-centeredness, self-service, self-assertiveness, pain, hurt, wounds, abandonment, and betrayal and nail it all to the cross of Christ.

We live our lives to proclaim our King, to

Crown Him Lord of years,
The Potentate of time;
Creator of the rolling spheres,
Ineffably sublime:
All hail, Redeemer hail!

For Thou hast died for me:
Thy praise shall never, never fail
Throughout eternity.

—"Crown Him with Many Crowns,"
Trinity Hymnal, 295

I sat next to the bed of my friend, John Ross. Oh, he had been more than just a friend. He was one of those blood brothers who had stood by me in the midst of everything the Lord had taken me through over a span of three or four years. He met with me, had lunch with me, cried with me, prayed with me, and constantly spoke words of encouragement and hope to me. Now, here he was in the throes of his last battle here on earth. John had been diagnosed with esophagus cancer, and just when the doctors thought they had removed it, the cancer returned and quickly brought him to his deathbed. They had sent him home to die.

He lay in the bed in his family room, not moving, not saying anything. I spoke words of warfare to him, but he did not respond. Then I said, "John, I am going to pray for you." Now, it seems at times like this, in the midst of sickness and impending death, that God's Spirit grabs hold of me and causes me to pray with greater power and passion than I normally do. I do not remember the exact words I began with, but as I stood, seeking to usher John into the presence of our great King, he—not yet having responded to me or anything I had said—raised his hand up high above his head. As I continued praying, I grabbed his hand, and he squeezed it as if saying, "Here we are before the King of kings and the Lord of lords! How great it is!" John went home to glory later that day. I wish I had possessed the chorus to that song, "One Thing Remains," to give to him.

> Your love never fails.
> It never gives up.
> It never runs out on me.

Kingdom living ends with our last battle here on earth. It is a process that begins the moment we are held in the grip of God's grace and brought into His Kingdom, and then we live out our lives, ever walking, running, fighting, trusting, and praying. What are we to remember in all of it? That we are the King's beloved! Kari Jobe sings:

"My Beloved"

You're my beloved; you're my bride.
To sing over you is my delight.
Come away with me my love.
Under my mercy come and wait
'Til we are standing face to face.
I see no stain on you my child.

I sing over you my song of peace.
Cast all your care down at my feet.
Come and find your rest in me.

I'll breathe my life inside of you.
I'll bear you up on eagle's wings
And hide you in the shadow of my strength.

I'll take you to my quiet waters.
I'll restore your soul.
Come rest in me and be made whole.

You're my beloved; you're my bride.
To sing over you is my delight.
Come away with me my love.

Amen, beloved! *Amen!*

About the Author

Dr. George W. Mitchell has a BS, MDiv, and Doctor of Ministry degree. He has been a senior pastor, executive pastor, and associate pastor of churches in Alabama, Georgia, and Florida. In serving these churches, he has written numerous Bible studies for small groups, leadership development materials, men's discipleship materials, and Christian education programs. He has planted two churches and established two Christian schools. Not only has he taught Bible and Latin in a Christian school, but he has been a professor at Birmingham Theological Seminary, teaching Apologetics, Systematic Theology, Old and New Testament Surveys, Worship, and Practical Theology, along with being the chairman of the Practical Theology Department and director of the Doctor of Ministry Program. Presently, he is pastor of the St. Luke Evangelical Church in Newton, Kansas. He has six wonderful children (including his daughters-in-law and his son-in-law) and five incredible grandchildren with another one on the way.

Forgiveness

Our Greatest Need,
Our Greatest Gift

Dr. George W. Mitchell